Towards a General Theory of Boredom

Through comparative historical research, this book offers a novel theory explaining the emergence of boredom in modernity. Presenting a Durkheimian topology of cross-cultural boredom, it grounds the sociological cause of boredom in anomie and the perception of time, compares its development through case studies in Anglo and Russian society, and explains its minimal presence outside of the West. By way of illustrative examples, it includes archetypes of boredom in literature, art, film, and music, with a focus on the death of traditional art, and boredom in politics, including strategies enacted by Queer intellectuals. The author argues that boredom often results from the absence of a strong commitment to engaging with society, and extends Durkheim's theory of suicide to boredom in order to consider whether an imbalance between social regulation and integration results in boredom. The first book to scientifically explain the historical emergence and epidemic of boredom while engaging with cutting edge political debates, *Towards a General Theory of Boredom* will appeal to scholars across the social sciences with interests in social theory, social psychology, and sociology.

Elina Tochilnikova is Visiting Researcher at Northeastern University, USA. Her research focuses on the intersection between emotional experience and culture, and its expression within the realms of psychopathology, art, and politics. Currently, she is designing digital games for the treatement of mental illness. She earned her PhD from the Department of Sociology at Boston University, USA.

Classical and Contemporary Social Theory

Classical and Contemporary Social Theory publishes rigorous scholarly work that re-discovers the relevance of social theory for contemporary times, demonstrating the enduring importance of theory for modern social issues. The series covers social theory in a broad sense, inviting contributions on both 'classical' and modern theory, thus encompassing sociology, without being confined to a single discipline. As such, work from across the social sciences is welcome, provided that volumes address the social context of particular issues, subjects, or figures and offer new understandings of social reality and the contribution of a theorist or school to our understanding of it.

The series considers significant new appraisals of established thinkers or schools, comparative works or contributions that discuss a particular social issue or phenomenon in relation to the work of specific theorists or theoretical approaches. Contributions are welcome that assess broad strands of thought within certain schools or across the work of a number of thinkers, but always with an eye toward contributing to contemporary understandings of social issues and contexts.

Series Editor

Stjepan G. Mestrovic, Texas A &M University, USA

Titles in this series

Fall Girls
Gender and the Framing of Torture at Abu Ghraib
Ryan Ashley Caldwell

Utopia
Social Theory and the Future
Edited by Michael Hviid Jacobsen and Keith Tester

The Social Pathologies of Contemporary Civilization
Edited by Kieran Keohane and Anders Petersen

Torture, Intelligence and Sousveillance in the War on Terror
Agenda-Building Struggles
Vian Bakir

A Sociology of the Total Organization
Atomistic Unity in the French Foreign Legion
Mikaela Sundberg

Sociological Amnesia
Cross-currents in Disciplinary History
Edited by Alex Law and Eric Royal Lybeck

Max Weber's Theory of Modernity
The Endless Pursuit of Meaning
Michael Symonds

David Riesman's Unpublished Writings and Continuing Legacy
Edited by Keith Kerr, B. Garrick Harden and Marcus Aldredge

Fiction and Social Reality
Literature and Narrative as Sociological Resources
Mariano Longo

C. Wright Mills and the Criminological Imagination
Prospects for Creative Inquiry
Edited by Jon Frauley

Diagnostic Cultures
A Cultural Approach to the Pathologization of Modern Life
Svend Brinkmann

Beyond Bauman
Critical Engagements and Creative Excursions
Edited by Michael Hviid Jacobsen

Ghosts, Landscapes and Social Memory
Martyn Hudson

Existence, Meaning, Excellence
Aristotelian Reflections on the Meaning of Life
Andreas Bielskis

The New Narcissus in the Age of Reality Television
Megan Collins

Depressive Love
A Social Pathology
Emma Engdahl

For more information about this series, please visit:
https://www.routledge.com/sociology/series/ASHSER1383

Towards a General Theory of Boredom

A Case Study of Anglo and Russian Society

Elina Tochilnikova

LONDON AND NEW YORK

First published 2021
by Routledge
2 Park Square, Milton Park, Abingdon, Oxon OX14 4RN

and by Routledge
52 Vanderbilt Avenue, New York, NY 10017

Routledge is an imprint of the Taylor & Francis Group, an informa business

British Library Cataloguing in Publication Data
A catalogue record for this book is available from the British Library

Library of Congress Cataloging-in-Publication Data
A catalog record has been requested for this book

ISBN: 978-0-367-48455-2 (hbk)
ISBN: 978-1-003-03984-6 (ebk)

Typeset in Baskerville
by Taylor & Francis Books

Dedication: This book is dedicated in loving memory of my grandfather Mikhail Khaykin (7.1.1925–11.12.2014) who always encouraged and inspired me to reach for the stars and to devote myself fully to the study of humanity and to my wonderful sister Liya Tochilnikova whose capacity for unconditional love, creativity, and celebration served as powerful motivation throughout my writing.

Contents

Tables

Acknowledgements

I want to begin by thanking my parents, Alla Tochilnikova and Boris Tochilni-kov, who made great sacrifices to encourage and support me to make my dreams of becoming an academic and author, a reality. Critically, I am greatly indebted to Neil Jordan, Alice Salt, and anonymous reviewers at Routledge for their enthusiasm, suggestions, and support throughout my writing process. Addition-ally, I am greatly indebted to my primary advisor John Stone whose intellectual brilliance, strength of character, belief in my study, and wonderful sense of humor proved invaluable throughout my project. He injected every interaction with meaningful suggestions and "the fun factor". I am also deeply indebted to Deborah Carr and Nazli Kibria who spent endless hours assisting me and my research and bringing my study into fruition. Their deep and useful insights and friendly attitude were invaluable and cannot be overstated. I am also indebted to Ana Villareal who met with me regularly in the embryonic stage of my study and pushed for more "real life" supporting case studies in institutions such as art, Joseph Harris who provided critical feedback on context and methodology, Ashley Mears whom I interacted with closely in the beginning stages of my sociology career and whose original study of the commodification of beauty and emphasis on methodology inspired me to explore niche yet highly relevant sub-disciplines of sociology, Alya Guseva who regularly sent me articles on boredom and whose kindness and friendliness encouraged me to continue in academia, and Emily Barman whose emotional support and suggestions during a difficult episode in my career proved invaluable. I am hugely indebted to Yuri Corrigan who helped me formulate my arguments vis-à-vis Russian society, literature, and poli-tics. He dedicated countless hours to our meetings and to editing excerpts on Russian society and to Eviatar Zerubavel at Rutgers University who offered many hours of invaluable guidance for studying the *unremarkable* and to Deborah Belle, a Professor and friend, at Boston University who, throughout my career, generously encouraged my study and helped me formulate a quality book proposal. I am also incredibly grateful to Gordon Fellman at Brandeis University, Andrew Bradley, Liam Carrol, and Mikhail Itskovich, who offered edits, paragraph by paragraph, on a significant portion of my work, with deep insights into the phenomenon of boredom. Without the mentioned names, this work would have been impossible.

Introduction

The democratic experience of the everyday

> It seems probable that the human capacity for being bored, rather than man's
> social or natural needs, lies at the root of man's cultural advance.
>
> Anthropologist Linton (1936)

Boredom is a common yet imprecise term which has rarely been placed under the
scientific microscope of clear definition and systematic analysis. It has been
defined as a state of suspended anticipation, free-floating attention, a desperate
search for something to do, restlessness, a state of lack, an unrelieved sense of
emptiness, being absorbed by a lack of absorption, purposelessness, and a rejection of an unsatisfactory present. Although we have all experienced boredom in
some capacity, we have rarely considered its social ramifications.

Preliminary findings suggest that boredom has reached epidemic proportions
(Benjamin ([1927–1940] 2002); Haladyn 2015; Klapp 1986) and has spread
throughout the workforce (O'Bannon 2017). Critically, scholars have posited that
boredom has been a major driving force for critical historical events: from catalyz-
ing world wars (Kustermans and Ringmar 2011; Rose 1965) and triggering terrorism (Haque et al. 2015) to birthing modern art (McDonough 2017) and leading
wake-to-sleep media consumption (Klapp 1986). Studies suggest that boredom
influenced Hitler's decision to partake in WWII (Kustermans & Ringmar 2011),
Adolf Eichmann to join the Schutzstaffel (S.S.) (Arendt [1963] 2006), the decline of
British colonialism (Aerbach 2018), youth to join ISIS (Haque et al. 2015), the
outcome of presidential elections (Frey, Berger, & Chen 2017; Frey Berger, & Chen
2018) and attraction to the charismatic rule of President Donald Trump and President Vladimir Putin (Bennetts 2018; Grove 2018; Jacobs 2018; Perper 2019;
Petroski 2018; Robinson 2018). Boredom has contributed to *indifference* emerging as
a political strategy (Peiss, Simmons, & Padgug 1989; Roth & Katz 2013; Cage
1973), modern art severing ties with traditional art and reinventing itself as a new
social institution focused on resolving modernity's existential crisis of meaning
(McDonough 2017; Haladyn 2015), and our addiction to consuming social media
while privileging it over interactions with people (Klapp 1986). Echoing Linton's
(1936) observation quoted at this beginning of this chapter, Western society is eco-
nomically and technologically 'progressing', as we acquire more access to resources
and opportunities, counter-intuitively, boredom is on the ascent, with more people

reporting feeling bored for more of their experience. For example, Google Trends (2019) shows that 'google searches' for the word "boring" doubled worldwide between 2004 and 2018. And while boredom has grown ubiquitous in the West, it remains virtually unknown in the rest of the world (Goodstein 2005): most languages lack the word and concept, and Western etymology only dates to the 17th century (Burton 2017). According to Google Trends (2019), between 2004 and 2018, few in Africa and China 'google searched' the word "boring". Although boredom is a major consequence of modernity and has become central to Western society, we know little about boredom's qualities, causes, influence in our lives, cultural boundaries, and spread. Without understanding boredom, we cannot understand modernity, its trappings and potential, and most importantly, modern society of the 20th and 21st century.

This book defines boredom, creates a Durkheimian topology of cross-cultural boredom and its sociological cause of anomie, and the perception of time, and compares its emergence and development through case studies in Anglo[1] and Russian society. Hence, I argue that social norms, guiding principles, and core values are essential for social adjustment and feeling engaged with society. Without a strong commitment to engaging with society, boredom may result. Additionally, this study extends Durkheim's *Theory of Suicide* to boredom and considers whether an imbalance between social regulation and integration may result in boredom.

Anglo and Russian society are presented as case studies for comparative analysis because of their fascinatingly divergent historical, cultural, religious, ideological, national, class, gender, economic, linguistic, and literary traditions, suggesting symbolic and emotional boundaries for culturally-specific experience. Each culture is founded on core values and norms with differentiation in institutional formation. Important dimensions of its cultural process, for example, individualistic or collectivistic values and social structure, are codified in its language. While in English "I" is presented with an upper case, in Russian, as in all other languages, it is presented with a lower case, demoting one's individualistic self and one's significance in mass society. The reification of the self in English and the demotion of the self in Russian, have profound implications for self-definition, social cohesion, and for the spread of anomie. In Anglo society, there is a bias towards anomie over stratification, whereas in Russian society, there's a bias towards stratification and social control over anomie. Bias towards anomie defines individualistic society whereas bias towards conformism defines collectivistic society.

Further historical differences define both societies. Unlike Anglo society, the Russian Empire was largely excluded from the influence of the Renaissance. Russia never experienced a comparable movement cultivating virtue, human achievement and genius, universal human rights driven-by humanism, individualism, skepticism, versatility (crystalized in the archetype of the Renaissance person), secularism, classicism, civic participation, reason and free will, focused on the dignity and capability of humanity. These orientations contrast with the pre-Renaissance values of monastic life, divinity of God, frailty of man, and dependence on God's grace, which characterized Russian society until the Russian revolution.

Additionally, Russian history contains several seemingly anachronistic and culturally-divergent elements. Slavery (serfdom) continued in Russia later than in other European countries and finally ended in 1861 (Moon 2001). While Britain had abolished slavery in 1834 and while slaves had composed approximately 8% of the US population[2] (United States Census Bureau [1860] 2018), an 1857 census reported that 37.7% of the Russian population continued to be enslaved. Additionally, Russia limited secularism, upholding its Byzantine legacy and the power of the Orthodox Church, maintained extremely limited civic participation and scientific activity. Communism further institutionalized countless non-freedoms and conformism, yet promoted secularism and an end to religion. During and following the collapse of the communist Soviet Union, there was a short period of seeming freedom and reconstruction (Glasnost and Perestroika). However, few of the freedoms experienced during this period were institutionalized. Importantly, unlike in Anglo society which experienced major issue-based social movements promoting counter-culture, environmental, racial, women's, gay, and human rights, the Soviet Union and Russia were excluded from comparable uprisings. Currently, Russia's political establishment promotes 'an imitation of freedom and democracy', while maintaining the fundamental elements of dictatorship and feudalism. More recently, its national structure has excluded Russia from the economic benefits of capitalism—most Russians continue to merely subsist (Shevstova 2013; Shevstova & Kramer 2013). I show that Russia's cultural context and legacy have profoundly affected Russians' consciousness and existential world view and produced its own unique variety of anomie.

In *The Lonely Crowd: A Study of the Changing American Character*, Riesman ([1950] 2001) implies that, divorced from culture, there is no authentic human nature. Cultures rest on fixed beliefs and characters; there are no absolutes. In order to underline the importance of culture for understanding symbolic experience and to highlight the nuances of culturally-specificity, this book compares anomie and the emotional phenomenon of boredom through the lens of two empirical scenes: Anglo and Russian society. It serves as a historical-comparative testament to cultural heterogeneity and its symbolic consequences. Each culture's members are both the captives and creators of their respective character.

Durkheim's concept of anomie

Durkheim's scholarship is unmistakably the foundation of sociology. Being the son of a rabbi, he likely understood the trappings of religion and philosophy in explaining social reality and sought to develop a true science of humanity. Both religion and philosophy can be reduced to a matter of personal belief and are teleological and tautological. There is no way to prove or disprove 'God' or philosophy as neither are subjects for scientific methodology; personal faith and ideology are choices. Critically, Durkheim was writing during a time of the mainstreaming and popularization of psychiatry and psychology. And yet, aware of their limitations, stewarded a new discipline: sociology. Psychiatry assumed that our mental dis-eases and functioning are an extension of our brain and in this respect, neurological and a subset of neurology. Whereas psychology's view was myopically focused on human functioning, apart from its natural context: environment and culture, dismissing critical cohesive and regulative influences. Neither could fully describe nor explain humanity's experience, dis-ease, and social ills. Durkheim charted a profound new discipline, one that captured humanity and society as *sui generis* and in which society, in terms of its subjective power over the individual, was the symbolic equivalent of God. This new discipline's focus was symbolic meaning-making and culture, the collective symbolic creation and renewal of meaning (emergent phenomenon), and unpacking the inherent tension between the individual and society. Durkheim's religious background drove his religious coloring of social ills in the language of the immorality and sin of unchecked and unlimited desire ([1897] 1979), the malady of the infinite ([1893] 2014), the morbid desire for the infinite ([1897] 1979), the bottomless abyss of emotions ([1897] 1979), and the inextinguishable thirst as constantly renewed torture ([1897] 1979). These associated phrases, which Durkheim described as accompanying experiences of anomie, have become synonymous with anomie.

Complementary to anomie, Durkheim developed two concepts for the tension between the individual and society: social integration and social regulation. In his new science, diseases could, at least in part, be reduced to social maladjustment and its mental sequalae. Durkheim's main explanatory concept, anomie, posited that poor 'social regulation'/unchecked desires are so consequential that they lead to suicide. He writes:

> Anomy, therefore, is a regular and specific factor in suicide in our modern societies; one of the springs from which the annual contingent feeds. So we have here a new type to distinguish from the others. It differs from them in its dependence, not on the way in which individuals are attached to society, but on how it regulates them.... The third sort of suicide, the existence of which has just been shown, results from man's activity's lacking regulation and his consequent sufferings. By virtue of its origin we shall assign this last variety the name of anomic suicide...In anomic suicide, society's influence is lacking in the basically individual passions, thus leaving them without a check-rein.... But economic anomy is not the only anomy which may give rise to suicide. The suicides occurring at the crisis of widowhood, of which we have already spoken are really due to domestic anomy resulting from the death of husband or wife. A family catastrophe occurs which affects the survivor. He is not adapted to the new situation in which he finds himself and accordingly offers less resistance to suicide. ([1897] 1979, pp. 258–259)

Furthermore, in his most famous and counterintuitive discovery, Durkheim demonstrates that Protestants have the highest suicide rate, followed by Catholics, and Jews. As during this epoch, Protestants had the most freedom and wealth, followed by Catholics and Jews, suicide rates were disproportional to freedom and wealth. His research was radical in that it empirically demonstrated that society matters. Additionally, it uncovered a specious Western ideology: freedom and wealth increase happiness, while tradition and restriction are dangerous. Hence, limitless personal freedom resulting from inadequate social regulation/ unchecked desire is not only gluttonous, but lethal.

The definition of anomie has become a point of debate. In *Suicide* ([1897] 1979, p. 258), Durkheim writes: "The state of de-regulation or anomy is thus further heightened by passions being less disciplined, precisely when they need more disciplining" meaning that anomie occurs with inadequate regulation. Although he did not use the term himself, anomie has often been translated and defined as *normlessness*. Describing the anomie of an unmarried man, Durkheim writes:

> he aspires to everything and is satisfied with nothing. This morbid desire for the infinite which everywhere accompanies anomy may as readily assail this as any other part of our consciousness; it very often assumes a sexual form… When one is no longer checked, one becomes unable to check one's self. Beyond experienced pleasures one senses and desires others; if one happens almost to have exhausted the range of what is possible, one dreams of the impossible; one thirsts for the non-existent. How can the feelings not be exacerbated by such unending pursuit? For them to reach that state, one need not even have infinitely multiplied the experiences of love and lived the life of a Don Juan. The humdrum existence of the ordinary bachelor suffices. New hopes constantly awake, only to be deceived, leaving a trail of weariness and disillusionment behind them.… The uncertainty of the future plus his own indeterminateness therefore condemns him to constant change. The result of it all is a state of disturbance, agitation and discontent which inevitably increases the possibilities of suicide. (p. 271)

He continues to describe anomie:

> moreover, all sorts of excesses, abrupt and violent changes in physical environment, disturb the organism, derange the normal play of functions and thus cause species of deliria during which the idea of suicide may arise and be put into effect. (p. 110)

In *The Division of Labor in Society* (Durkheim and Coser [1893] 2014) Durkheim continues to imply his definition of anomie:

> For anomy to end, there must then exist, or be formed, a group which can constitute the system of rules actually needed. Neither political society, in its entirety, nor the State can take over this function; economic life, because it is specialized and grows more specialized every day, escapes their competence and their action. (p. 11)
>
> [...]
>
> If the division of labor does not produce solidarity in all these cases, it is because the relations of the organs are not regulated, because they are in a state of anomy. (p. 287).

Anomie's quality of a lack of regulation has led many functionalist sociologists to translate anomie as 'normlessness' or deregulation. However, Durkheim never used these terms himself.

Many scholars have grappled with anomie's etymology and its English equivalent. In the preface to *The Division of Labor in Society* (Durkheim & Coser 2014) George Simpson writes:

> To translate Durkheim's term "anomie" I have called back to life an English word obsolete since 1755 and first used in 1591, anomy. The Shorter Oxford English Dictionary finds it used in its earlier period to mean "disregard of (divine) law", and in its later, "lawlessness".... The adjective of this noun which Durkheim uses, "anomique", has no English counterpart, obsolete or current, and I have had to coin a word which I hope gains some currency because of its fullness of meaning. That word is anomic.

Anomie offers no direct translation into English. Mestrovic (1993) posits that the concept has been misconstrued by mistranslation and poor conceptualization by functionalists:

> I demonstrate that Durkheim never wrote of anomie as normlessness, but as a state of collective evil or derangement characterized by a painful state of infinite desires that are never satiated. Here again, Durkheim's and particularly rabbinical heritage probably played a role in sensitizing him to the idea that society itself can be evil: anomie becomes the secular counterpart of the religious notion of sin (Mestrovic 1985a).... This problem goes beyond the structuralist-functionalist misinterpretation of anomie as a pathological distortion that lies at the periphery of society and affects only its deviants. Rather, in Durkheim's original intent, anomie afflicts society at its core. And an anomic society hides its collective sickness from itself. As such, the remedy for anomie requires radical social restructuring which can occur only after the neurotic society achieves collective insight into its affliction. One has only to think of the dramatic social problems in today's postmodern societies, from violence to the near extinction of the family, to appreciate the relevance of Durkheim's conceptualization of anomie as collective derangement over the insipid and useless functionalist notion of "normlessness". (p. xiii)

Mestrovic (1993) continues to emphasize that one of the only synonyms that Durkheim explicitly used for anomie was *dérèglement*:

> "Normlessness" and "deregulation" are poor translations of *dérèglement*, for several reasons. First, they did not enter common English usage until the 1960s and certainly did not exist in Durkheim's time.... *Dérèglement* is difficult to render in English ... it is perhaps best translated as derangement ... expressing two nuances of moral disorder: What is dérangé is disarranged ... or is without place. What is *déréglé* is out of rule. (pp. 62–63)

Durkheim's discussion of *dérèglement*, connoting religion, focuses on insatiability of desires, uncontrolled appetite, inextinguishable thirst, evil, immorality, undisciplined passion, restlessness towards an indefinite goal, impatience, suffering, and destruction. He notes anomie within the spheres of the economy, politics, marriage, religion, and the intellect.

One of Durkheim's colleagues, Jean-Marie Guyau, whom he read and reviewed, wrote on anomie in *The Non-Religion of the Future* ([1897] 2017, p. 248) and defined moral anomy as "the absence of any fixed moral rule, the complete enfranchisement of the individual in all religious matters.... Instead of accepting ready-made dogmas, we should each of us be the makers of our own creed". Hence, Guyau's definition of anomie as no fixed rule overlaps with Durkheim's. However, unlike Durkheim, who identified anomie as fatal, Guyau's stance emphasized the empowerment of its individualistic qualities.

Riesman ([1950] 2001) applies Durkheim's anomie to understand a primary issue in modernity: characterological maladjustment and its social consequences:

> In each society those who do not conform to the characterological pattern of the adjusted may be ... anomic.... Durkheim's anomique (adjective of anomie) meaning ruleless, ungoverned. My use of anomic, however, covers a wider range than Durkheim's metaphor: it is virtually synonymous with maladjusted.... In determining adjustment, the test is not whether an individual's overt behavior obeys social norms but whether his character structure does. A person who has the appropriate character for his time and place is "adjusted" even when he makes mistakes and does things which deviate sharply from what is expected of him.... Conversely, just as nonconformity in behavior does not necessarily mean nonconformity in character structure, so utter conformity in behavior may be purchased by the individual at so high a price as to lead to a character neurosis and anomie: the anomic person tends to sabotage either himself or his society.... Thus, "adjustment", as the term is used here, means socio-psychological fit, not adequacy in any evaluative sense. (p. 242)

Like Riesman, I am less interested in the *act* (imitation) of adjustment or anomie and more interested in subjective experience: in what ways to do historical subjects feel well-adjusted or anomic? The paradox of acting adjusted while experiencing anomie speaks to society's pressure to externally conform. The cost for pretentious external conformity is anomie.

Informed by Durkheim's description of anomie, his synonymous use of the terms *dérèglement* and *déréglé*, as well as the above theorists' analysis, I conceptualize anomie as social and moral lawlessness of unchecked desires which, in line with Riesman's ([1950] 2001) conceptualization, I term and simplify as 'characterological maladjustment'. As humanity necessitates an instinctual need to 'fit in', when there is a mismatch between one's character and societal needs, anomie follows as a symptom of not fitting in. It is synonymous with societal anarchy in which one is no longer restrained by institutional, traditional and moral scripts, often leading to the grave social consequences of fragmented identity, restlessness and greed for endless undefined goals, few meaningful connections, misery, and boredom.

Although Durkheim neither explicitly explored, nor explained boredom, Klapp (1986) infers how his theory connects to Durkheim's concept of anomie as discussed in *The Division of Labor in Society*:

> Concerning ritualism as a form of anomie takes us back to Emile Durkheim, who theorized in a way that helps explain boredom produced by *variety*... Durkheim held that anomie, loss of social regulation, exposes people to a range of choices ungoverned by rules of fixed status, a pursuit of novelties that is not only demoralizing but frustrating and boring.... disintegration of social bonds, especially rapid rises of status, remove needed constraints from the individual, opening him to boundless desires and insatiable striving which result not in happiness but boredom. Anomie gives rise to "greed", also a thirst "for novelties, unfamiliar pleasures, nameless sensations, all of which lose their savor once known". The pursuit of such pleasures is endless and futile. (p. 47)

Durkheim mentions boredom three times in the text and never states its connection with anomie. Overlapping with boredom, the text discusses desensitization and loss of pleasure and happiness that result from superficial and endless novelty-seeking. Although Klapp (1986) tangentially mentions that there is a relationship between anomie and boredom, he fails to explain, elaborate, and provide evidence for such a relationship and to integrate anomie into his theory. Additionally, he suggests that identity problems and anomie are synonymous[3], whereas I posit that anomie offers a hermetically-sealed concept with significant causal power for it explains boredom as well as identity problems. This study makes a case for anomie driving boredom. Klapp's (1986) theoretical framework provides supporting types and examples.

Simple versus existential boredom

According to a broad consensus in the literature and to my case studies of Anglo and Russian society, there are two main types of boredom: simple common boredom and complex existential boredom. *Simple common boredom* is usually experienced as unpleasant waiting and is characterized by a lack of will or complacency and by the attitude of withdrawal.

Importantly, unpleasant waiting interacts with class and is often symptomatic of poverty while being able to shorten waiting is often symptomatic of wealth. Many shortcuts exist for the affluent: personal assistant services, shoppers, drivers, banking, chefs, concierge, and private physicians, pilots on privately charted airplanes, VIP membership with priority entrance, amongst other short-cuts and time savers, while being poor is associated with waiting in long-lines and on waiting lists for financial assistance, housing, medical care, transport, and for discounts. Although the affluent may experience less simple common boredom, they likely experience more of the existential variety, as will later be discussed. Critically, unpleasant waiting intersects with power dynamics. In professional settings, inferiors are more prone to wait for superiors than vice versa. While, housewives often spend time waiting for their husband to return home and offer them attention, as will be discussed in the *Temporality* section. Hence, although boredom is ubiquitous and democratic, its particular style is felt along class and power lines.

Simple common boredom is experienced from childhood throughout the life-span resulting from predictable, monotonous, repetitive, and inescapable circumstances such as subjectively valueless tasks. Simple boredom is correlated with administrative regulation and its archetypal experience of waiting, which characterizes modern society. Goffman ([1967] 2017) in his writing on symbolic interactionism complicates and personalizes such an experience:

> boredom, too, can occur during unfocused interaction, as we may observe in almost any queue of individuals waiting to buy a ticket. And just as agencies such as alcohol and marijuana may be employed to transform a conversation into something that is not embarrassing or boring, so these may function to put individuals at ease in the wider scene provided by unfocused interaction. Just as a witticism may do honor to the conversational moment, so the wearing of new or special clothing, the serving of rare or costly food, and the use of perishable flowers can draw attention to the unique value of a wider social occasion. (pp. 133–134)

He emphasizes that waiting in a queue, although generally held as an experience of boredom or unfocused interaction, which he sees as interchangeable through the process of *symbolic interactionism*, can assume countless meanings. Hence, there is no human experience that necessarily holds any value or meaning. We imbue our experiences with meaning through our interaction with society and simple boredom, even in a stereotypically monotonous experience, may or may not result depending on the meanings assigned by the individual.

Simple boredom can also be driven by a sense of corporeal satiation and excess, as when one is stuffed with food and can no longer tolerate eating but has not chosen any alternative activity. Framed differently, achieving complete satisfaction with the only activity you can think of wanting to do and not being able to think of any alternative, leads to simple boredom. This experience can turn into a chronic state of apathy, entrapment, and malaise. *Complex existential boredom* is a philosophical affliction driven by extended aimless waiting—a sense of emptiness and meaninglessness which may result in the search for meaning. Existential boredom is a dehumanizing state as it deprives one of meaning. Viktor Frankl (1975) explains the root cause of existential boredom:

> Unlike an animal, man is no longer told by drives and instincts what he must do. And in contrast to man in former times, he is no longer told by traditions and values what he should do. Now, knowing neither what he must do not

what he should do, he sometimes does not even know what he basically wishes to do. (p. 91)

Hence, as animals are driven by instincts, they do not have to consciously make choices and find meaning in their experience. Humans, however, are part animal, but for whom instincts have become secondary, to cultural meaning-making systems, in driving behavior. Through our evolution, we have become *primarily* cultural beings for whom tradition and ritual, as well as possibly the hallucinating 'bicameral mind' (Jaynes 1976) were driving forces in behavior. In modernity, tradition and ritual have fizzled and been replaced with openness and freedom—the two breeding grounds for anomie, which in turn led to boredom.

There are several important distinctions between simple and existential boredom. The most basic distinction is being bored *by* versus being bored *with* something. Or from another perspective, existential boredom is the apogee of simple boredom. They can be conceptualized sociologically by the categorization of anomie and time (from temporary to chronic inertia; with a focus on the present):

A focus on the present is essential for boredom to emerge, as will be explained fully in the *Temporality* section. In brief, every emotional dis-ease is characterized by a time-focus. Importantly, when we feel some element of dis-ease, we notice time and begin looking at the clock and fidgeting. Whereas, when meaningfully occupied, subjective time disappears. Subjective awareness of time is associated with anomie and the disappearance of subjective time is associated with emotional well-being and social adjustment. The above time-orientations are ideal-types, in the spirit of Weber, and most expressions of emotional dis-ease are mixed types.

Kierkegaard ([1843] 2009) wrote that the melancholic lives in memory and that the path to happiness is repetition (ritual); without healthy repetition, one's life will dissolve into meaningless noise (anomie). Referencing Becket, Svendsen (2005) writes:

> The only thing that exists is time, too much time, in a universe where nothing has happened.... To be set to wait for a moment that will never come, in a world of immanence, with no outside at all. This is boredom taken to its logical conclusion. (p. 99)

In line with Kierkegaard and Becket, depression is characterized by a regretting and ahistorically living in the past. While anxiety is characterized by a fear of and largely living in the future. Those bored, live in the prison of an unsatisfying present, lacking meaningful activities and rituals. They're unable to reflect on the past or plan for a more pleasing future. Quoting Milan Kundera, Svendsen (2005, p. 135) writes: "The degree of slowness is directly proportional to the intensity of memory; the degree of speed is directly proportional to the intensity of forgetting". Kundera implies that with contemporary society's pace of life, invoking meaningful memories becomes harder. Without such memory, the mind becomes too localized on the current empty moment and painful atrophy results—as simple or existential boredom. "Boredom is reminiscent of eternity, where there is no transcendence. Time collapses, implodes, into a vast, empty present" (Svendsen 2005, p. 127). Interestingly, subjective time slows both for those bored and for those shocked/traumatized, suggesting that boredom and shock/terror are not polar but adjacent experiences. For example, many popularized reports describe watching a train hit a passerby and subjectively experiencing time as slowing or stopping. Linguistically, in Russian literature, political analysis, and culture, boredom and terror have been conceptualized as overlapping adjacent experiences (Bellow [1975] 2008). My study implies that the temporal structure of experience is culturally, emotionally, and circumstantially shaped. Temporality is an important contribution largely ignored by Durkheim.

Table 0.1 Anomie and time leading to simple and existential boredom

Limited period of time **[Focus on the present]**	**Ongoing period of time** **[Focus on the present]**
↓	↓
Anomie → Simple common boredom	Complex existential boredom

The above categorization (Table 0.1), based on anomie and temporality, implies that simple boredom and complex boredom are the same type of experience and may be viewed on a continuum. Simple boredom is easier to tolerate because of its implicit expectation that it's time-limited and will end soon. Additionally, there may be a collateral expectation of necessity as in the case when one waits in line for medicine to cure oneself. The believed necessity of the situation makes it tolerable. However, if simple boredom is prolonged enough, experienced on a daily basis, and extended to enough spheres of life, it can progress to complex existential boredom. For example, if one is in solitary confinement for a day, one will likely experience simple boredom, but if one's punishment is extended long-enough, one will likely go mad with existential boredom; long-term confinement leads to madness (American Psychological Association 2012). Another example involves 'busy work': if you have to spend a few days completing futile and laborious tasks, it may result in simple boredom, whereas if you're aware that busy work will monopolize your lifelong career, and the activity of most days, you may fall prey to the existential boredom (soul-deadening) of "what is the point of all of this?" and consider resigning. Hence, time-limited unpleasant activity, if extended, may lead to existential boredom.

The simple boredom of waiting can transmute into spiritual suffering. The latter type of boredom is more painful and intolerable as sufferers find it difficult to justify the experience. The regular conditioning and anticipation of 'boredom' enters one's belief system and permeates one's existential experience of "my life is empty and such emptiness is unbearable". Often, sufferers wonder about the point of feeling constantly bored and dissatisfied and struggle with imbuing their experience with meaning and purpose. The experiences of those afflicted with existential boredom may be conceptualized as part of 'the psychopathology of everyday life' under the umbrella of psychiatry. Existential boredom is commonly expressed in the following musings; "Maybe I should be at a different point in my life by now…", "Maybe I should have achieved more…"; "Maybe I need to be doing more towards my future…". Such musings may lead to acute suffering and insanity if their root conflict of identity formation and social maladjustment is not resolved or if (as above) conditions of sensory deprivation, such as solitary confinement, are extended. If the root conflict or situation of sensory deprivation remains unresolved, one experiences life as a solitary confinement of existential boredom and such a state eventually becomes unbearable and leads to insanity (American Psychological Association 2012).

Another important temporal distinction is between length and pace. Waiting is often experienced as unpleasant, not because of its objective length, but because of its subjectively jarring pace and realization of powerlessness over time. Svendsen (2005) writes that when we are bored, we often find ourselves watching the clock, which on its own, is not a pastime, but a sign of boredom and restlessness for time to move faster:

> At the same time, it is worth noting that it is not the objectively measurable length of the watch's time that is linked to boredom, because it is not the length but rather the pace of time that is of importance. (p 118)

Yet, with prolonged length, time's pace begins to feel unpleasant. Whereas, as discussed, when we are occupied, time subjectively disappears or slows. Subjectively forgetting time is a strong metric for the polarities of boredom: social engagement and enjoyment. This is 'the' reason most of us seek constant occupation. Time is one prominent way of distinguishing between the two boredoms, however, their most essential distinction is one of consciousness. In simple boredom, one anticipates an end, while in existential boredom one feels imprisoned and hopeless that their state will continue indefinitely.

Let us consider the theoretical framework of sociologist Orrin E. Klapp (1986, p. 119), a social structure theorist, who developed a metaphorical theory of boredom, conceptualizing the phenomenon along four quadrants:

Table 0.2 Boredom along four quadrants

Good functional redundancy	Meaning	Good variety
1	↑	3
Redundancy ←		→ Variety
2	↓	4
Boring redundancy	Entropy	Boring variety

Source: Klapp (1986). Reproduced with permission of Greenwood Press Inc.

Klapp's theory was hugely influenced by Viktor Frankl's *Man's Search for Meaning*, Weber's concept of modern *disenchantment*, and Durkheim's concept of anomie. His theory conceptualizes boredom as the result of inadequate or surplus information. Boredom is framed as the opposite of personally-meaningful information (entropy), variety of information, and redundancy. When meaning and redundancy are combined, one experiences *good functional redundancy* (1): no boredom. In this quadrant, information is meaningful and redundant: dependable, secure, safe, referencing collective tradition, ritual, memory, educational, and following useful rules. Celebrating a Wedding anniversary with close ones and playing tennis are two common examples. When redundancy and entropy are combined, one experiences *boring redundancy* (2): boredom. This is achieved with the repetition of common-sense and non-useful information such as banality, mindless repetition, monotony, dogma, and stagnation. Such information is repetitive and offers nothing new and is lacking in utility and meaning. Contexts such as Beckett's *Waiting for Godot*, where little changes, are breeding grounds for such structural boredom (Klapp 1986). When meaning and variety are combined, one experiences *good variety* (3): no boredom. This is experienced as discovery, innovation, inspiration, amazement, awe, and can be achieved through learning, exploring, adventuring, inventing, and playing games. When variety and entropy are combined, one *experiences boring variety* (4): boredom. This is experienced as chaotic disorganized noise, irrelevant information, confusion, and information overload. In fact, Klapp's (1986) four types of boredom are caused by anomie.

When a new experience emerges and spreads, neologisms emerge to capture and efficiently communicate such experience. The historically-novel idioms of 'killing time', 'time consuming', 'keep busy', 'beat the clock', 'make up for lost time', 'bite off more than you can chew', and 'burnout', and the recent acronym neologisms of FOMO and YOLO capture our society's and, particularly, my generation's existential boredom. FOMO stands for the "fear of missing out" while YOLO stands for "you only live once". Both millennials and generation z (those born in the 1990s) ubiquitously reference FOMO and YOLO communicating their angst of missing out on the wonderful experiences of life. They report that whatever they are doing, they often imagine doing something more enjoyable and worthwhile. As their focus is on an upgraded imagined reality, they fail to fully invest in their current experience, rendering their current reality not fully worthwhile and quite boring. Importantly, both acronyms speak to a sentiment of fear and regret around meaningful time-usage. Whereas the noted idioms emphasize that we have begun valuing, quantifying, and evaluating our use of time as well as become a society biased towards action in an effort to avoid time-waste and boredom. In fact, the conspicuous consumption of time through busyness has become a status symbol (Belleza, Paharai, & Keinan 2016) For many, this leads to accepting more responsibility and activity than one can reasonably handle. Hence, efforts at avoiding time-waste and boredom often result in burnout.

The Western experience of existential boredom is interesting in that it notably contrasts with the pre-boredom historical period (the majority of humanity) and with most non-Western cultures which lack language and concepts for boredom (e.g. Hindi, Gujarati, Cantonese, Mandarin, Ghanaian). In many non-Western cultures, references to circumstances and experiences which would commonly be framed as boredom in the West, are framed as meaningful, spiritual, peaceful, and entry points to connection with the self, to 'flow'[4] (Csikszentmihalyi 1990), the universe (often referred to as "The Great Void"), and to spiritual awakening. Such cultures also ascribe strategies for 'working with' emptiness and void, precluding anomie and the emotionally jarring "Western" boredom. For example, in Hinduism, the feeling of emptiness and such inner void are often framed as critical elements of an ideal spiritual state where one realizes the emptiness of all experiences and achieves a sense of oneness with the universe (Kempton 2014). This simulates the common experience of gazing into the great void of the night sky and feeling peaceful awe. Hence, in many other cultures, people aspire to the state of emptiness and to feeling inner void. In such cultures, simply being present and quietly spending time together is considered natural, peaceful, and lovely. The absence of an activity or goal is a sign of harmony and closeness and does not lead to boredom. Many non-Western cultures enjoy and appreciate experiential states of non-doing, quiet, and peace. Framed differently, such cultures imbue the experiential state of emptiness with meaning precluding anomie and the jarring experience of boredom.

This reflection is especially striking when we consider that many languages lack a future tense and do not lend themselves to the frustration of 'waiting'[5] (a future focused experience which may lead to *simple boredom* and *existential boredom*), planning, and imagining future time with goals and comparing oneself to one's imagined future self. To reiterate, many cultures which do not have language for boredom imbue similar experiences, such as emptiness, with meaning, and lack an emphasis on linear time and a focus on the future. Emotional experiences are culturally-bound (different cultures have different experiences, hence the existence of the disciplines of cultural sociology and anthropology): it may be hard for non-Western cultures to even imagine, let alone experience 'our' boredom, just as it would be for us to esteem emptiness and inner void. As boredom has not emerged and spread throughout most of the non-West, its unprecedented and peculiar historical emergence in the West warrants explanation.

Temporality

The inclusion of a temporal variable was influenced by Simmel ([1903] 1969), Goodstein (2005), and Johnsen (2016). Simmel wrote of the "subjective temporal schema" (Goodstein 2005, p. 6) of time in reference to the change in the subjective experience of temporality with modernization and its referent shift from traditional to mechanical time. Mechanical time may be easily imagined through the experience of railway travel which is often described as rolling space during which anticipating the destination dominates. Hence, our changing experience of space-time created the possibility for boredom to emerge. Haladyn (2015) writes:

> In industrialized modes of transportation time becomes the definer of distance rather than the other way around, making the destination of travel an all-important end that makes the required time spent in accomplishing this task—as well as the experiences that occur during this period—simply a waste, something to be killed or filled up with distractions. (p. 56)

Although 'time travel' need not be boring as it can be filled with amusement such as reading, games, and movies, most see commuting and traveling long-distances as a wasteful nuisance or necessary evil.

With modernity, the experience of time accelerates and acquires new meanings,[6] causing impatience and boredom. We begin "privileging expectations over experience", where anticipating certain outcomes takes precedence over experiencing the current moment (Haladyn 2015, p. 65). Haladyn writes:

> Much of the literature on boredom highlights the relationship between our consumer-based culture and the apparent decrease in people's attention spans, which in all likelihood is the result of the promotion of disposable objects and constantly changing interests (often treated positively by referring to them as 'trends'). As a result, our desires are typically satiated only temporarily when treated to new forms of stimuli. We expect to be constantly entertained, so much so that we judge every aspect of our daily lives in terms of how it holds our interests – experiences that do not promise immediate engagement are quickly labeled 'boring'. (Ibid., pp. 2–3)

Hence, temporal expectations and attention spans have shifted; contemporaneously, we expect immediate gratification and fast-paced stimulation in the form of consumption and entertainment. Other experiences are dismissed as boring. Goodstein (2005, p. 127) emphasizes that modernity reifies the use of time for 'progress' and upholds a moral prohibition against wasting time. Zerubavel (1981), describing a novel modern phenomenon, writes:

> An *activity cult*, whereby people are expected to maximize their "active" time and to minimize any "empty unaccounted-for" time periods". (p. 56)
> [...]
> Many people today are becoming specialists in the fairly sophisticated art of "killing time", which involves filling otherwise "empty" and unaccounted-for time intervals such as riding on the subway or waiting in a lobby with "fillers"—with newspapers and magazines. (p. 58)

There is a tendency to solve one's fear of running out of time by multi-tasking and engaging in multiple activities simultaneously (Zerubavel 1981), with increased value given to time, acceleration of consumption, and simultaneous consumption (Linder 1970).

We have become sensitive to a 'lack of time'/'running out of time', and in line with this, it is our personal responsibility to choose the causes that are worthy of our progress and to select 'non-wasteful' activities. However, no matter the choice we enact, we can always imagine a more worthy cause or a more beneficial use of our time, often leaving us regretful and guilty. Johnsen (2016, p. 2) writes: "In boredom, time appears to stand still, unable to pass" because we have failed to imbue time with meaning and importance. It seems that although, with modernity and its industrialization, we acquired speed and efficiency, we lost the romanticism of the present moment and the joy of living a life in slow motion. Gardiner and Haladyn (2017) observe that modern time is characterized by novelty-seeking behavior:

> As for the ever-accelerating dynamic of novelty itself, it is hardly news. The normalization of change under a universalized rhetoric of innovation or even unending revolution, the assiduous production of an appearance of incessant change that amounts to an ever-fluctuating, eternal return of the same … just such a fashionable re-packaging of old wine into new bottles. (p. 24)

Such a normalization of change has led to a culture seeking distraction and hyperactivity.

We have also begun privileging media over in-person human interactions. Klapp (1986) describes modern society:

> a system in which … people literally get up and go to bed by media … plugged into telephone, television, radio, cassettes, computers, film, credit-card transactions, and all the rest most of the time, on the job, in their cars, on the way to and from work, and at home. They hustle to keep up with information … a dependency that some experts do not hesitate to call addiction … it does not take long for media people … to be unsure whether additional amounts of information make them all that better off. (p. 6)

This description echoes even louder in our current internet and smartphone world where most people cannot imagine their life unaided and unorganized by consuming media, yet unsure of the net-sum benefit of living in such a society. Although media can be consumed deliberately and meaningfully, many use it because they're unsure of how to occupy themselves otherwise. Media consumption has become a filler for unorganized time and an addiction. The current style of wake-to-sleep consumption is being utilized as a major distraction from boredom (see Chapter 5). Such ubiquitous efforts at distraction signal a societal crisis. This suggests that capitalism exploits boredom to encourage consumerism and may have been birthed as an extension of boredom. It may also suggest that political institutions, including representative government and extremist groups such as ISIS and neo-fascists, which sustain themselves by utilizing social media, may exploit 'the bored' for their own purposes.

In terms of temporality, it is important to emphasize that every functional mental dis-ease is partially-driven by a focus on the past, present, or future. Those who are depressed, live in and regret the past while those who are anxious live in and fear the future; both are in a state of temporal misalignment. Boredom, which until now, has been conceived as a symptom of mental dis-ease but not an illness in its own right, is *driven by the present*. For those bored, both the past and the future seem too far off to feel relevant and they are unable to imbue the present with compelling content. The radical presence they experience, without past or future projections, feels painfully vacuous. Hence, boredom is the disease of indifferently, unimaginatively, and idly living in the present. A strong example of boredom being present-driven is found in the experience of temporality in the Soviet Union. Jerphagnon (1997) as quoted by Narusyte (2010, p. 130) writes: "The constant decline in economic and social conditions did not allow for optimism for the future; time seemed to be 'frozen' into an inalterable present where human life passed meaninglessly". Soviet citizens, having been denied religion, spirituality, free and flexible participation in society, and a better future, were often limited to living in the grey monotonous present.

Different historical periods and societies have different temporal rhythms, and when one's personal experience of rapidity is different from one's societal expectations, this division proves jarring and may be experienced on the spectrum of over-stimulation/chaos to under-stimulation/boredom. Although it is important to note that the acceleration of temporality positively correlates with the ubiquity of boredom, this is only due to anomie's ascension in modernity. If acceleration took place in a rigidly stratified society, where the foundational values, rules, scripts, and ascribed meanings did not vary, such as within the ancient Indian caste system, anomie, and its symptom of boredom would not result. *In my causal theory of boredom, anomie plays a primary role while temporality plays a secondary role*. This is an essential emphasis. Boredom emerges in anomie even in situations without accelerated temporality, such as in the case of Anna Karenina's lover Count Vronsky who experiences pangs of boredom while living in the countryside, or in the case of Indian society, which even contemporaneously has maintained its norms and has not fallen into anomie, although its pace of life has accelerated in line with modern globalization, industrialization, and capitalism.

Cultural variability

My findings suggest that although boredom is driven by anomie and results from social maladjustment, its experience diverges in Anglo and Russian society. In the Anglo case, sufferers tend to experience difficulty in defining themselves and in choosing their life calling, belief system, and daily activities. They're bored because they feel that they don't know themselves well. Consequently, they struggle assessing their life direction and preferences. Applying Riesman's ([1950] 2001) typology and assessment, Anglo society has become other-directed, while

Russian society has become inner-directed, as will be discussed later. According to Riesman, other-directed persons, famously noticed by de Tocqueville ([1835] 2002) on his visit to America and described by Veblen ([1899] 2009), are a radically new type of man, friendly yet uncertain of himself and demanding approval from others. Their values, standards, and behavior are guided by reified others in their generation, either known personally or through mass media; as opposed to their ancestors (Riesman [1950] 2001). They are conformist and sensitize themselves to follow others' signals for direction and validation of approval. Their primary struggle is autonomy and maintaining an autonomous life: with influence, their goals can easily and often change as they focus on compulsive adjustment. 'Keeping up with the Joneses', which has become 'keeping up with the Kardashians', and insatiably and anxiously desiring to be liked monopolizes their experience. Their self-drive and preference for independent thought and action is limited. They chose to symbolically mutilate aspects of themselves that do not sit well with societal expectation.

This case is well-depicted in Betty Friedan's well-known "Feminine Mystique" ([1963] 2013) who captures the experience of post WWII suburban American housewives. To more fully describe her subject, she quotes psychiatrist Margaret Sanger:

> She has no identity except as a wife and mother. She does not know who she is herself. She waits all day for her husband to come home to make her feel alive. And now it is the husband who is not interested. It is terrible for women, to lie there night after night, waiting for her husband to make her feel alive. (p. 75)

The depiction of American housewives as not knowing themselves, outside of their husbands' identities clearly serves as a supporting case for the other-directed archetype and its partner of Anglo style of boredom. Sanger further elaborates (Friedan [1963] 2013):

> ... by never achieving the hard core of self that comes not from fantasy but from mastering reality, these girls are doomed to suffer ultimately that bored, diffuse feeling of purposelessness, non-existence, non-involvement with the world that can be called *anomie*, or lack of identity, or merely felt as the problem that has no name. (p. 267)
> [...]
> housework was endless, and its boring repetition just did not give that much satisfaction, did not require that much vaunted expert knowledge. (p. 312)
> [...]
> The woman with two children, for example, bored and restive in her city apartment, is driven by her sense of futility and emptiness to move, "for the sake of the children", to a spacious house in the suburbs. The house takes longer to clean ... routines are so time consuming that, for a while, the

emptiness seems solved. But when the house is furnished, and the children are in school … "there is nothing to look forward to", as one woman I interviewed put it. The empty feeling returns so she must decorate the living room… Yet none of it is quite as real, quite as necessary, as it seems. (p. 345)

[…] The housewives who suffer the terror of the problem that has no name are victims of the same deadly "dailyness". As one of them told me, "I can take the real problems; it's the endless boring days that make me desperate". Housewives who live according to the feminine mystique do not have a personal purpose stretching into the future. But without such a purpose to evoke their full abilities, they cannot grow to self-realization. Without such a purpose, they lose a sense of who they are. (p. 433).

The 'girls' Friedan describes are young women resigning themselves to the drudgery of domesticity and marriage, manipulated into an anomic life filled with empty, repetitive, and unsatisfying chores, while remaining disconnected from a life of developing their unique gifts and capacities and maladjusted to the social sphere outside of the home. They make a virtue out of necessity and artificially create domestic tasks to fill their void, while remaining aware of the inherent meaninglessness of their routine. Sometimes, as in the example of housewives and their social circles of the 19th century silver spoon literary genre (also known as the fashionable novel genre), boredom is framed as a status symbol: "Rank has its bores as well as its pleasures" (Disraeli [1845] 2017, p. 90). In this case, boredom is deliberately emphasized and enacted as a status achievement with housewives feeling they've reached their social peak by being born or marrying wealthy and no longer having to do anything *at all* (except for signaling their boredom to one another to affirm their identity and class membership). They deny their will and the possibility of creating meaning in their lives (Goodstein 2005, p. 58). These women typically spend their days lounging while deliberately opting out of occupation, with one exception: letter writing. They write their family and friends long tedious accounts of their non-activity and slow passing of time, emphasizing boredom. While the capitalist engine pumps drive and motivation into most, they afford the simple living of remaining still and diverting to a life of being in the moment and fleeting observations. Even in such cases where vacuous identity development and *conspicuous boredom* are framed as a status symbol, subjects suffer from its suffocation.

This study coins the term conspicuous boredom which is defined as: maintaining the appearance of boredom in an attempt to enhance one's prestige and involving a philosophy of 'doing nothing'. This may in fact be a symptom of the psychopathology of affluence, as will be explored throughout this study, and is in line with Veblen's ([1899] 2009) famous *The Theory of the Leisure Class* in which he identifies conspicuous consumption. Besides for the privilege of wealth, high status, and a high quality of life, those of the leisure class, because of who they are and what they stand for, have the privilege of 'anything' they 'do or experience' being framed as fashionable and esteemed. The converse is the case for those who are considered 'low class' and disreputable. Hence, even the boredom of the elite becomes fashionable and their blasé is reified and imitated. Conspicuous boredom is only possible in hierarchical societies with a leisure class, and therefore, has not been identified as a phenomenon in Soviet Russian society.

Boredom assumes a different experience and re-enactment in Russian society. Unlike in the Anglo example where sufferers feel bored from the emptiness of not knowing themselves and the resulting paralysis of executive functions, Russian tedium tends to result from a mismatch between the sufferer's unshakeable identity and her disapproving environment. Riesman's ([1950] 2001) archetype of inner-directedness captures the orientation of the Russian-style of boredom. Inner-directed persons are radically self-driven and focused more on character and aligning their behavior to their principles, rather than on personality, pleasing others, and on popularity. As they have a strong sense of self coupled with relative insensitivity to external trends and opinions, inner-directed people have the capacity to achieve a stable sense of self and stability in their greater life (Riesman [1950] 2001). Importantly, inner-directed personalities are not culturally-relativist. Their belief systems are quite stable, and they tend to be savvy at deconstructing and reinterpreting their culture to suit their needs.

Collaterally, they tend to struggle with interpreting and integrating societal expectations and may struggle with adaptation and experience episodes of resentment, resistance, and rebellion. "They may refuse to adapt because of moral disapproval of what the signals convey. Or they may be discouraged by the fact that the signals, though inviting enough, do not seem meant for them" ([1950] 2001, p. 33). Their historical archetypes are captured in the role of the nobles, priests, and wandering artists. As they aren't behaviorally-focused and thus, struggle with conformism, they scrutinize the gap between their characterological weaknesses and societal potentialities. Riesman elaborates ([1950] 2001):

> the inner-directed child must be taught to fly a straight course away from home, with destination unknown; naturally many meet the fate of Icarus. Nevertheless, the drive instilled in the child is to live up to ideals and to test his ability to be on his own by continuous experiments in self-mastery—instead of by following tradition. (p. 42)
> [...]
> They tend to feel throughout life that their characters are something to be worked on. The diary-keeping that is so significant a symptom of the new type of character may be viewed as a kind of inner time-and-motion study by which the individual records and judges his output day by day... The relative uncomfortableness of the more powerfully inner-directed homes—the lack of indulgence and casualness in dealing with children—prepares the child for the loneliness and psychic uncomfortableness of such questions and of the social situations that he may confront ... the child's character is such that he feels comfortable in an environment which, like his home, is demanding and which he struggles to master. (pp. 44–45)

Focusing on self-mastery, those inner-directed are more prepared for and comfortable with struggle than their outer-directed counterparts.

Riesman ([1950] 2001) explores the tragedy of the inner-directed person of reaching for the stars while being confronted with real-world limitations:

> Yet there is often tragedy in store for the inner-directed person who may fail to live up to grandiose dreams and who may have to struggle in vain against both the intractability of the material and the limitations of his own powers. He will be held, and hold himself, to his commitment. Satirists from Cervantes on have commented on this disparity between pursuing the stars and stumbling over the mere earthiness of earth. (p. 116)

The most famous such case is illustrated by Tolstoy's Anna Karenina. Anna, while married to a man she loves platonically, falls in passionate love with another. Throughout the novel, she remains unshakably resolute about her desire to divorce her husband and to re-marry her lover. Her knowledge of herself and her desires is unquestionable,[7] yet her nontraditional morality does not fall neatly into Russian convention. Anna's strong character, gusto, and desiring of more than what society can offer are matched by a rigid social structure which pushes back on her every initiative. Her echelon polices her efforts of self-realization and a stalemate ensues. Anna must choose between living with her soul mate or remaining in society. Either choice, living together in isolation or living separately, yet in society, would leave both her and her lover miserable and bored. She's unable to make a decision and goes mad. The results are tragic: the novel ends with Anna losing her son and committing suicide, and her lover leaving for war expecting to die.

The Soviet epoch provides another fascinating case study of the Russian-style of boredom. Narusyte (2010), a proponent of different social circumstances leading to different expressions of boredom, describes the Soviet context:

> Yet the causes of social boredom were very different in this totalitarian country where life was structured around ideological slogans and where the central planning of the economy made competition obsolete and every attempt to free thinking, especially concerning religious issues, was punished ... boredom was identified with an unwillingness to conform to the rules set by the authorities, and even social resistance against the system... the conditions of boredom were specific behind the 'iron curtain' ... first of all, while Western societies suffered from an overload of information and change that created the impression that life was ephemeral, Soviet society and its social environment could be described as boring in the sense that it simply lacked variety; it was uniform and nothing changed throughout the decades. (p. 129)

Every culture has its trademark atmosphere, rhythm, emotion, and behavior; uniformity, monotony, boredom, fear, and rebellion, respectively, may have categorized Soviet culture. As most 'stuff' was rationed and there were virtually no stores, people's stuff was quite uniform. The 1975 comedy *The Irony of Fate*

(Eldar Ryazanov) was an ironic commentary on uniformity being so extreme that one can mistake another's home for one's own. That being said, many Soviet citizens who emigrated to the US found their new life boring compared to their life in the Soviet Union where they worked in their chosen profession and maintained a rich cultural, intellectual, social, and personal life (Orleck 1999). In cosmopolitan centers, variety did not come from 'buying stuff' or consuming opposing media sources, but from reading literature, poetry, learning about the arts, attending concerts, theater, opera, and engaging in many social exchanges with family and relatives (who generally saw each other and spoke on the phone, frequently), neighbors (who lived in communal settings), friends (with whom very close emotionally intimate ties were maintained), colleagues, and others.

Although there certainly was boredom during the Soviet Union, it took place in anomic moments, situations, and pockets of society and was not the norm. In general, Soviet society was so hugely regimented and challenging to survive that most likely did not take to boredom. Few cases of boredom were recorded during the Soviet Era (see Chapter 5).

Since, the decline of the Soviet Union, anomie and boredom have increased. Mestrovic (1993) comments on institutional anomie and post-communism help clarify anomie in Russian society:

> Western economists began to export consumer-based capitalism to nations that are still reeling from the collective pathology engendered by the communist experiment. Durkheim's writings lead one to predict that the introduction of infinite consumption—already problematic in the West—to nations whose institutions such as the family, professional groups, and religion have been weakened by communism is an invitation to rampant anomie. (pp. xiii–xiv)

The fall of the iron curtain resulted in anarchy, chaos, a rise in criminality and violence, as well as the implementation of state-sponsored capitalism and the rise of newfound consumerist values. From Riesman's ([1950] 2001) conceptualization, it can be inferred that Russia transitioned from inner and tradition-directed behavior to an other-directed behavior.

Boredom as an art strategy

One of the most fascinating supporting cases for anomie driving boredom is found in the modern art world. Artists such as Andy Warhol and John Cage deliberately enacted boredom as an art strategy with the dual-goal of echoing the anomie of modernity and encouraging individual meaning-making. They rejected traditional art and enacted a completely novel strategy that was more social activism than fine art, and although it neither completely took off nor succeeded in its goal of empowering its audience to master anomie, it was a fascinating attempt at triggering self-awareness and empowerment. Haladyn

(2015) diagnoses the issue of boredom in modernity to which modern art powerfully responded:

> The problem of boredom is not the experience of a lack of interest, which speaks to one's failed ability to be fascinated or feel a connection with one's life; boredom in its affirmative state functions to establish just such a link. Rather, it is through a profound lack of fulfillment that subjective will is confronted with its own limit, forced to extend itself—beyond mere interest, yet dependent upon a passionate interest—to the extremity of its power. The 'boredom' we are discussing is clearly more than its common or colloquial usage, the term defining not just a minor personal problem but also and more importantly a subject's experiential lack of meaning within modern life. It defines a borderland of affective experiences that confronts us with, rather than distracting us from, the crisis of meaning in modern culture. As such, what boredom in fact describes is the subjective lack that is at once the cause and result of being bored. Boredom calls upon us, inciting us to look into this meaninglessness that refuses to give a purpose or a final goal to life, leaving us at the mercy of our own subjective causality ... to create meaning out of the meaninglessness of life in this merely subjective world. (pp. 4–5)

Andy Warhol famously responded by reifying everyday objects such as his famous Campbell's soup can and experiences such as trying on clothes as inherently worthy of attention and personal meaning-making. In the end, art has become a commodity just like his prints.

Influenced by the West, an interest in producing deliberately boring art spread to the Soviet Union (Narusyte 2010). Just as their Western counterparts, Soviet artists reflected their own monotony by regularly invoking the theme of boredom in aesthetic representation. One well-known contemporary example is that of conceptual photographer Boris Mikhailov who seeks to depict the daily lives of the homeless. Effimova (1994 as quoted in McDonough 2017) writes:

> By the end of the 1970s the rigidly congealed space of Soviet society appeared to show signs of dissolving. Emigration, dissent and widespread cynicism highlighted the growing incongruity between the social ideal and the discrepant reality. The incongruity became more and more visible, saturating the landscape: the contrast between the weary, tired faces of the passers-by and the monuments exuding great enthusiasm, between the pathetic, dilapidated interiors and the grandiose facades, between the greyness and blandness of everyday life and the crimson banners that stretched along the streets. The specifically Soviet elements of culture no longer seemed integrated into life but stood out like deeply familiar yet alien oddities. (p. 182)

Mikhailov's mostly black and white photography aims to capture this visual and cultural disintegration through common Soviet scenes of gloomily marching in political demonstrations and selling pastries for survival in front of grand communist monuments.

Soviet conceptual artists, as their American counterparts, struggled to make sense of their newfound anomic experience of their society dissolving and people's mindset changing. They applied art to capture their observations. However, compared to the American *Aesthetic of Indifference* which confronted audiences with a boring experience (see Chapter 3), Soviet conceptual art captured the boring spaces and mindset of its people in order to construct a narrative and trigger political change. It was confrontational and dangerous, and it led to many being beaten, imprisoned, and exiled abroad.

The boredom of politics

This study explores boredom within the realm of politics and representative government. I establish a relationship between boredom versus engagement in the electorate during episodes of war and relative peace. Georges Perec (1967, p. 58) poetically describes post-WWII emptiness as living in "prisons of plenty" which captures my conclusion that it is psychologically more exciting to live in a state of war and psychologically blasé to live in a state of peace. Electoral boredom is connected to supporting extreme political figures, and grand and 'meaningful' war efforts. This study applies Arendt's ([1963] 2006) concept of the *banality of evil* to historical cases of participation in violence and places the stance of 'no opinion' within Queer politics. Importantly, this chapter demonstrates that populism in the age of social media is an antidote for those who are bored, marginalized, or feel that their opinions do not have a home.

A study reviving the democratic experience of the everyday

Pioneered by sociologists Henri Lefebvre and Guy Debord, this research serves to revive the study of everyday life which currently remains incognita in the Academy. I remind social science that the mundane serves as the background of the novel. It is inherently critical, interesting, and worthy, as its study could lead to a greater understanding of ourselves and to social transformation. The majority of available scholarship focuses on the supposedly superior experience of specialized activities and on the sensational, extreme, easily entertaining and palatable. Yet, social research fails to capture the most democratic and encompassing: the majority of our daily experience. Investigating the everyday is the most democratic and authentic focus as it assumes primacy in our lives and is universal. While few achieve the 'great' and while many experience emotional intensity such as depression or panic, all of us encounter the banal and boring in some capacity. And yet, such focus in sociology is virtually nonexistent. Sociologist Walter Benjamin, who participated in the Parisian College of Sociology, writes ([1927–1940] 2002, p. 105): "We are bored when we don't know what we are waiting for. That we do know, or think we know, is nearly always the expression of our superficiality or inattention. Boredom is the threshold of great deeds". Benjamin observes that understanding the often-overlooked state of boredom may lead to attention, seriousness, depth, and great accomplishment.

In his famous Arcades Project ([1927–1940] 2002) he emphasizes that in the 1840s boredom emerged as an epidemic, caused by urbanization and mechanization, and became the characteristic trait of modernity. Gardiner and Haladyn (2017) interpret Benjamin's writing:

> Being bored provides a means of allowing both individual and society an imaginative mental space, away from the proscribed meanings given on the surface of life's experiences, one that culturally and historically is needed for the possibility of accomplishing great deeds. He questions the basis of our ability to recognize meaning in life. (p. 11)

Boredom is a potentially productive and empowering state that allows us to deeply reflect on prescribed meanings and consciously and deliberately make personal choices.

In his speech presented speech at the sociological conference organized by The Group for Research on Everyday Life, Guy Debord (1961) encourages sociology to gaze more closely and systematically at the 'insignificant' and often excluded moments of our lives:

> if people censor the question of their own everyday life, it is both because they are aware of its unbearable impoverishment and because sooner or later they sense—whether they admit it or not—that all the real possibilities, all the desires that have been frustrated by the functioning of social life, are focused there, and not all in the various specialized activities and distractions. Awareness of the profound richness and energy abandoned in everyday life is inseparable from awareness of the poverty of the dominant organization of this life.

Inquiry into boredom is essential as it remains 'the' characteristic emotion of modernity, as it comprises the common and seemingly insignificant moments of our contemporary lives. Whereas in pre-modernity, religious devotion may have imbued the everyday with significance, in modernity, echoing Brodsky (1995), boredom imbues our lives with insignificance and reminds us of our inner void:

> For boredom speaks the language of time, and it is to teach you the
> most valuable lesson of your life—the lesson of your
> utter insignificance.

Without understanding boredom, we cannot understand modernity, its trappings and potential, and most importantly, modern society of the 20th and 21st century. Boredom remains the revolution modernity needs to conquer.

Notes

1 Anglo refers to English-speaking society. Any research published about English-speaking society and all literature originally written in English will be considered as possible data. The working assumption is that language shapes our processing of content, thinking, and experience of the world. As reflected in the data, native English speakers and native Russian speakers have qualitatively different symbolic experiences.

2 According to the US Census of 1860, 8% of the American population were slaves.

3 Klapp (1986) does not explain how they are synonymous.

4 Flow is a state in which the mind and body is so absorbed in an activity, that self-consciousness and one's sense of time disappears, the present is intensified, and one forgets oneself.

5 'Waiting' can lead to both simple and existential boredom. The former case is self-explanatory while the latter case may be imagined through the complaints of the psychopathology of everyday life: "I should be at a different point in my life by now", "I should have achieved more by this point in my life", "I need to be doing more towards my future".

6 Common new meanings are captured by famous proverbs such as "Lost time is never found again" (Benjamin Franklin), "Time is money" (author unknown) and "Time is what we want most, but what we use worst" (William Penn). These new meanings convey the awareness of time as a finite valuable resource and the fear of wasting it.

7 This is not Tolstoy's point, but my interpretation. Tolstoy is a conservative and is concerned with Russian culture falling apart from Western European influence. He implies that Anna is operating from a place of Western European influence (tropes of personal freedom and romantic love) and self-delusion. Operating from her delusional state, she rejects traditional Russian values and is therefore corrupted. He emphasizes that deconstructing traditional morality ends tragically. Tolstoy views personal authenticity and choice as invasive Western pathologies.

1   Definition

Qualities and types

Boredom generally refers to an emotion of apathy and low arousal with a lack of either notable positive or negative feelings. It also refers to the state of "feeling weary because one is unoccupied or lacks interest in one's current activity" (Oxford Dictionaries 2019) or to "feeling tired or unhappy because something is not interesting or because you have nothing to do" (Cambridge Academic Content Dictionary 2019). Hence, boredom is a defining emotion of disconnection with oneself and with one's context, which results in a state of vacuous apathy, the awaiting of something imprecise, and potential irritability. As all emotions and moods, it has a captive quality which confronts you, often without your consent. When boredom dictates, one feels powerless to transcend it.

Qualities and types

Boredom has several elements (Goetz et al. 2013): 1. Emotional or affective (unpleasant feelings) 2. Cognitive (altered perception of time and attention (Eastwood et al. 2012). 3. Physiological (reduced arousal) 4. Expressive (Facial, vocal, postural; although there is no universal facial expression for boredom (Ekman 1984)) 5. Motivational (alter or depart the situation). Each element can be conceptualized as being driven by anomie. When one lacks guiding principles, the resulting disorganization and confusion results in unpleasant feelings of irritation and emptiness, conceptual confusion, inability to concentrate, disconnection and disinterest (reduced arousal from the inability to connect), facial, vocal, and postural expressions of boredom (these vary and overlap with expressions of disinterest and irritation such as zoning out and fidgeting), and the drive to change or leave the situation. As one's impatience is proportional with one's sense of time and time's finality, the acceleration of everyday life leads to a sense of intense and urgent motivation to change or leave boring situations. In economic theory, this motivational element has been coined as the 'opportunity cost' of a situation. The historicity of subjective temporality and a prohibition against boredom implies that cultural tropes hugely influence emotional experience.

Klapp (1986) explains that since a changing sensory environment is essential for healthy mental functioning, boredom can also be driven by satiation, habituation, and desensitization. These states result from sensory overload and lead to a loss of awareness and a deadening of arousal. In modernity, these states occur simultaneously and interact. Klapp (1986, pp. 38–39) writes: "The overload of violence in the media is a case in point. Does the excitement of violence compensate people in real life? Does it satiate, hence appease the appetite for violence? Does it habituate people, so that they don't even notice how violent the media are?" Hence, boredom is composed of multiple interacting qualities.

There is much debate in the literature on whether delimiting boredom into types is meaningful. In their widely circulated study, Goetz and Frenzel (2006) identify four types of boredom according to the level of arousal and type of emotional affect: 1. Indifferent boredom; characterized by relaxation and withdrawal. 2. Calibrating boredom; characterized by uncertainty and receptivity to change or distraction. 3. Searching boredom; characterized by restlessness and active pursuit of change or distraction. 4. Reactant boredom; characterized by high reactivity and the motivation to leave a situation for alternatives. Reactant boredom is passionate and often involves yelling and complaining about one's boredom. Goetz et al. (2013) added a fifth type: Apathetic boredom characterized by learned helplessness and may be indicative of depression. Their framework implies that the catchall term of boredom conceals heterogeneous emotional states and motivations. However, the majority of scholars view boredom as a homogenous state, as will be discussed.

Extending Durkheim's theory of suicide to Goetz and Frenzel's (2006) categorization of boredom, besides for too little regulation, too little integration, surplus of either in society can also cause boredom. This argument is based on the assumption that human beings require a balance of regulation and integration; a balance between society and the self. Imbalance causes social maladjustment and, as an extension, imbalance may cause various symptoms from suicide (as Durkheim famously demonstrated) to boredom (as my comparative historical analysis suggests).

It is important to emphasize that most real-life examples will be mixed types. Inadequate regulation may lead to either calibrating or searching boredom as both are categorized by uncertainty and either a receptivity to or a search for change. In this type, one lacks regulation or guidance from one's environment as to how to proceed and is desiring of and searching for such guidance. Both calibrating and searching boredom may be conceptualized as subtypes of anomic

Table 1.1 The influence of imbalanced integration and regulation on boredom

Inadequate regulation	*Inadequate integration*	*Surplus regulation*	*Surplus integration*
Calibrating boredom[1]	Indifferent boredom[2]	Reactant boredom[3]	Apathetic boredom[4]
Searching boredom[5]	Reactant boredom	Indifferent boredom	Indifferent boredom
= Anomic boredom	= Egoistic boredom	= Fatalistic boredom	= Altruistic boredom

[5] Searching boredom: characterized by restlessness and active pursuit of change or distraction; overlaps with Durkheim's conception of anomie.

boredom. Contemporary suicide bombers and those who joined ISIS may serve as an archetypal example of inadequate regulation leading to a mixed type of calibrating boredom of receptivity to ideas and a searching boredom of looking for solutions. Most who became suicide bombers could not fit well into regular society and were rejected by the mainstream. This left them uneasy, not meaningfully occupied in their society, and likely bored. Thousands were recruited by ISIS and left to Syria to fight and die for a mission greater than themselves. Hence, anomic boredom may express itself as global terrorism. This one example signals the motivational potential and global consequences of boredom.

Inadequate integration may lead to either indifferent or reactant boredom; when one does not feel integrated, they may respond by become reclusive or by searching for alternatives. Both indifferent and reactant boredom can be conceptualized as subtypes of egoistic boredom. As with inadequate integration, surplus regulation may also result in indifferent and reactant boredom which can also be conceptualized as subtypes of fatalistic boredom. An example of surplus regulation leading to reactant boredom (fatalistic boredom) is found in Durkheim's description of slave revolts which were driven by the attitude of: "There's nothing there to live for. I might as well revolt" (Durkheim [1897] 1979, p. 276).

As both inadequate integration and surplus regulation can lead to indifferent and reactant boredom, this may suggest an inconsistency of Durkheim's framework. There may in fact be *little difference in the effect of regulation and integration,* and the categories may overlap. Through cases of cross-cultural boredom, this study will attempt to resolve the inconsistencies of Durkheimian theory and will offer a useful alternative. Lastly, surplus integration may lead to apathetic and indifferent boredom which can also be conceptualized as subtypes of altruistic boredom. Surplus integration can lead to someone losing their sense of self as expressed in the suppression of one's subjective will for the 'greater good', leading to apathy and indifference. A prominent example of surplus integration can be imagined through the Greek mythological case of Sisyphus who spent his life aimlessly rolling a boulder up a hill. Again, as inadequate integration, surplus regulation, and surplus integration can lead to indifferent boredom, this may suggest that the differences between integration and regulation are marginal. It is important to view the above categories as ideal types which can only be approximated and may overlap. The most common type of boredom is likely a mixed type.

Scholars have identified a range of nuanced emotional states of boredom. Hence, while one's boredom may be most punctuated by feelings of disconnection and emptiness, another's boredom may be expressed in a rejecting volition: "I don't want to do that!" The specific emotional nuance of one's boredom would be driven by one's context (organizing principles) and expectations. Julian Jason Haladyn (2015, p. 5) refers to simple boredom as "a trivial or inconsequential moment of detachment" and to existential boredom resulting from a crisis of meaning, and leading to "the question of will":

> boredom is not simply an aberration to be passed over as trivial but rather an integral component in the very fabric of life in modernity... boredom and

modernity are intimately connected through the subject that experiences life as a state of waiting for it knows not what, of being confronted by a world that is not given but rather encountered as a refrain. (p. 49)

Haladyn also comments on boredom's temporal quality: "The duration of boredom is in the fact of being bored, of an inability to be engaged or absorbed in the present, of an incapacity to obtain a vision beyond the self-conscious mediations that separate self from world" (p. 64). In line with psychoanalytic literature, he conceptualizes "the will to boredom", emphasizing that "boredom represents the possibility of creating meaning" making it an inherently valuable experience. Henry (2013), thinks of boredom as an affective state "in which unemployed energy is revealed to oneself. At each moment in boredom, a force emerges; it inflates by itself, and stands ready. It is ready for whatever use one would like to make of it" (p. 109). Antonio Calcagno (2017) reflects on Henry's definition:

On one hand, boredom manifests affectivity, life and the force to potentially create one's self and culture and, on the other hand, it is a failure to deploy the energy, force and revelations that boredom brings, resulting in an alienation from oneself. It is this latter failure that brings about the feelings of malaise, timelessness, dissatisfaction and ennui that we typically associate with boredom ... one can remain trapped in the positive aspect of one's boredom (i.e. one feels or undergoes life, affect or auto-affection), neither externalizing or creating oneself nor substituting an outside object or content as a result of the failure to deploy boredom's creative force. Boredom, then, becomes the pure feeling of the force to potentially create: one always feels that one is on the cusp of actualizing something, one constantly feels the force of the feeling of needing to deploy, but neither substitution nor creation/external articulation occur. (p. 54)

Hence, boredom is the emotion of unrealized potential, without a clear path for realization.

Phillips (1993) defines boredom as "that state of suspended anticipation in which things are started and nothing begins, the mood of diffuse restlessness which contains the most absurd and paradoxical wish, the wish for a desire" (p. 68). Boredom is a transitional state "akin to free-floating attention" (p. 69). While, O'Brien (2014) emphasizes:

Boredom is in part a volitional state, one having something to do with will and desire. To be bored by something is to want (i) not to have to deal with it, attend to it, listen to it, etc., but rather (ii) to do something, maybe anything, else instead. (pp. 238–239)

Hence, boredom is an expression of thwarted desire; although those bored may not feel their boredom in this way. It can also be experienced as an emptiness and absence that is painful to endure and as a lack of identification or an inability of knowing oneself: "When I'm bored I don't know myself!" (p. 70). In boredom, both the world and the self are experienced as poor and empty and one is involved in a desperate search for something to do; this may be a projection of an inner void or of a vacuous sense of self. O'Brien's (2014) description of boredom is in line with complex existential boredom.

Viktor Frankl (1986, p. 109) offers another compelling view of existential boredom as productive. He writes that inactivity and the inability to "fulfill the demands place upon us by our tasks" cause boredom. He implies that boredom is adaptive and important as it helps us maintain meaningful activity and to fulfill the demands of our lives. Calcagno (2017) interprets Frankl's work:

> Boredom, for Frankl, **is a result of the frustration of one's inherent will to meaning**. Meaning arises when one's own conscious intentionality for meaning, which is found in the will to meaning, meets up with an external meaningful object that fulfils and satisfies the meaning intention of the subject. The adequation of meaning fulfilment of the subject with the object results in the dispersion of the vacuum of existential boredom. Here, **we have the classic notion of boredom understood within a traditional cause–effect logic.** The internal experience of boredom is remediable through the coincidence of subjective and objective meaning. (p. 58)

Frankl's definition supports my theory of anomie leading to boredom.

From the child's perspective, boredom is the malaise of "having nothing to do" (Phillips 1993, p. 68) or being absorbed "by his lack of absorption" (p. 72), a state of waiting to find desire, and a crisis that is critical to the child developing the capacity to be alone. He emphasizes that it is important to allow children and to take care to not pressure children to be constantly *interested* and *interesting* as it takes away from their natural process of self-discovery. "But as adults boredom returns us to the scene of inquiry, to the poverty of our curiosity, and the simple question, What does one want to do with one's time?" (p. 75) and serves as a risk of making the right choice. He also identifies boredom as a defense against the unpleasant experience of waiting, that makes waiting tolerable and protects against rage. Hence, it's a hard reduction mechanism. "So the paradox of the waiting that goes on in boredom is that the individual does not know what he was waiting for until he finds it, and that often he does not know that he is waiting" (p. 78). Phillips (1993) further states that there are *many boredoms* including a multiplicity of moods and feelings. Each boredom is a mood with a point of view and with its own cause and motivation. However, he fails to identify and delimit the various types of boredom, their causes, and motivations.

Most scholars of boredom agree on its general definition yet differ on their take of boredom's relevance to childhood development. Toohey (2011), whose conceptualization is in line with Phillips, writes that boredom is a common human emotion as well as a philosophical affliction. He notes that those who are physically satiated are more prone to boredom than those who are starving. He delimits the term into two types: "simple" and "complex or existential boredom".

Simple boredom results from predictable, monotonous, repetitive, and inescapable circumstances (Eastwood et al. 2012; Fisher 1993; Wyatt 1929). Long speeches, meetings, church services, holiday dinners, and subjectively valueless tasks are examples.

Toohey (2011) emphasizes that giving a dull task value can mitigate its boringness. Simple boredom is common in childhood and throughout the lifespan. Complex or existential boredom is "a powerful and unrelieved sense of emptiness, isolation and disgust in which the individual feels a persistent lack of interest in and difficulty with concentrating on his current circumstances" (p. 1971). It overlaps with simple chronic boredom, depression, and feelings of apathy, disgust, and entrapment and is synonymous with world-weariness and ennui. Toohey (2011) claims that boredom is an adaptive emotion that helps humans thrive by protecting our sanity from unpleasant and unneeded social situations. Hence, boredom protects us from entering into situations of emotional dis-ease.

Svendsen (2005) emphasizes that boredom, besides for functioning as an emotion, is also a mood. He describes boredom as a mood that extends from maladjustment:

> we have cognition of a situation by virtue of the mood through which the situation is given to us. A mood is ... in the actual polarity that exists between humans and their surroundings.... A mood makes some experiences possible, others impossible. It conditions how ... all objects and events— appears to us.... Different moods give us different experiences of time, but also different experiences of space ... boredom differs from most other moods by the fact that the possibilities withdraw. (pp. 111–113)

He reminds us that the boredom's mood alters our temporal perception and leads to mental and behavioral paralysis. He then continues to describe boredom as an anomaly: "Boredom is mood which is reminiscent of an absence of moods. Since the mood is essential for our relation to objects, and boredom is a kind of non-mood, our relation to things also becomes a kind of non-relation" (p. 129). As boredom is characterized by the inability to authentically connect with one's environment, this is a critical emphasis.

Goodstein (2005) conceptualizes boredom as purposelessness and a rejection of an unsatisfactory present. It is experienced as both an empty meaningless time and as a "restless and productive discontent which fuels the motor of progress" (p. 101). She emphasizes that boredom cannot be understood apart from its linguistic expression. Synonyms include: ennui, langeweile, tedium, fatigue, blaseness, malaise, and 'a dull time'. It refers to both a "temporal elongation and to an existential state" (p. 107). Hence, boredom can be experienced as an unpleasant waiting or as spiritual suffering.

Spacks (1995) characterizes boredom as an idea, as a personal grievance or term of disapproval, and as a focus of opposition and social commentary:

> As an all-purpose designation of pain, the idea of boredom, while declaring the world inadequate, also subtly acknowledges our own insufficiency.... The

tension of lassitude with the wish to accomplish, of active impatience with stultifying dullness, infects our perceptions and thus makes a vivid world tiresome.... Boredom, unlike weariness, carries intimations of despair. (pp. 10–11)

Hence, boredom is an unpleasant experience which makes us feel inadequate, impatient, and tired. While, Anton Zijderveld (1979) conceptualizes boredom by its symptoms:

It can be observed that speech becomes gross and hyperbolic, music loud and nervous, giddy and fantastic, emotions limitless and shameless, actions bizarre and foolish, whenever boredom reigns. A bored individual needs these irritants of body, psyche and mind because he is not behaviorally stimulated in any other way (p. 77; cited in Spacks, 1995, p. 19).

Hence, those bored will seek extreme and even jarring forms of stimulating to quell their discomfort. Likely this has to do with desensitization to stimulation and desiring more stimulation for entertainment.

Definition

In English, boredom can assume countless meanings depending on its context and tone. Without context and tone, its meaning is vague; it is an unclear catchall term that has been diluted and lacks nuance, and shares no real synonyms. Not one generally considered synonym of boredom: listlessness, weariness, apathy, jaded, monotonous, tedious, doldrums, dullness, drabness or disillusionment capture the experience and its cause. One would say "I'm bored" but would rarely say "I'm disillusioned" or "I'm apathetic", or use any of the respective 'synonyms' of boredom to express their sense of lack of engagement. Each synonym captures one possible characteristic of boredom, yet misses boredom's essential emotional and temporal quality, and certainly lacks popular usage. For example, 'doldrums' means nothing is happening, yet fails to fully capture the experience or cause of boredom. Dullness is likely the closest to a synonym as it could imply a boredom based on lack of excitement and a lack of being drawn to something. But one would not say "I'm feeling dull". Jaded means one is disillusioned or desensitized, yet one may feel jaded but not bored. One could describe something, but not oneself, as monotonous. Similarly, one could describe a task, but not oneself, as tedious. Morrissey (2007, p. 160) writes "the modern English word does not catch its full range of meanings. More than just a feeling of tedium, dullness, and monotony, boredom can also denote a metaphysical world-weariness". This serves as a relevant contrast, when compared to boredom's synonyms in other languages.

Although in English there is no other word to describe the common feeling of boredom, boredom's meaning remains loose. For example, if a child says "I'm bored", the meaning is vague. One could be bored for a multitude of reasons and could express boredom throughout one's childhood, while one's close ones would not know why one is bored, and whether it is pathological and dangerous. It may be that 'bored' is vague on purpose, possibly to maintain the status quo, keep up appearances, or maintain politeness. Interestingly, unlike in Russian,[1] a lot of presumed synonyms for boredom in English are generally unavailable to children. In contemporary usage, labeling something as boring is often contrasted with labeling something as interesting. Such a way of simplistically and superficially communicating has become common and may suggest that people's thoughts have become as simple as their expression.

Measuring boredom is important for identifying and capturing its experience. Sixteen scales have been published for measuring boredom, however they diverge in terms of taxonomy, causality, and measurement, resulting in an aporia. Ontologically, these scales differ in terms of conceptualizing boredom as a personality trait versus environmentally-driven. The former scales are based on the assumption that people may carry the 'boredom trait' and no matter the context tend to low arousal and boredom; they are affectively sensitized to unstimulating situations and respond strongly, preferring situations of high arousal. For example, Wilson et al'.s (2014) study concluded that subjects, especially men, prefer pain to boredom and choose to experience electric shock rather than sit unstimulated and alone in a room for 15 minutes. This finding may suggest that the opposite of boredom is not necessarily interest or thrill, but intensity.

Those who explain boredom by environment believe that boredom is context-based, such as an extension of surplus leisure time or during unappealing work or sex. The two prominent and most utilized are the Boredom Susceptibility Scale (BSS) and the Boredom Proneness Scale (BPS). BSS assumes that individuals who are prone to boredom feel a need for regular external stimulation such as social interaction, activities, and entertainment, and measures one's desire for such stimulation. Hence, it uses sensation-seeking as a barometer for boredom and conceptualizes boredom as a personality trait. However, its validity is flawed. First, boredom may not be driven-by inadequate external stimulation. Second, the propensity to experience boredom may not be a stable personality trait. Third, BSS captures one's 'susceptibility' and not one's actual experience and current level of boredom. Fourth, this scale may capture susceptibility to the common boredom of waiting in line yet it is unlikely to capture the existential or complex boredom of painfully struggling to connect with one's context. It could be argued that in today's technologically-connected world of constant stimulation, sensation seekers would be easily satisfied engaging on their phone while waiting in line and less likely to experience common boredom than in the pre-technology era. While common boredom has likely declined due to technology, existential or complex boredom is on the rise due to secularization, globalization, competition, and the loss of sustainable life-long socially cohesive communities, as well the loss of clear social roles and expectations. Therefore, any boredom scale should capture and measure: 1. Boredom directly without using a correlative variable such as sensation-seeking. 2. Actual and current experience of boredom. 3. Common boredom versus existential/complex boredom. 4. Its cause/trigger. To reiterate, due to

BSS's validity flaws, it is neither helpful in capturing nor predicting one's experience or propensity to be bored.

The Boredom Proneness Scale (BPS) is similar to the BSS in that it measures the likelihood one is to experience boredom, yet, additionally, it attempts to assess transient versus chronic boredom. BPS's measurements are based on the assumption that boredom is adaptive as a transient emotion but harmful as a chronic state. Hence, it distinguishes those who experience transient versus chronic boredom. Transient boredom is common while chronic boredom is rare and pathological (Boden 2009). There are several benefits to transient boredom: having better educational and professional performance and more self-driven (Bench & Lench 2013) and introspection (Mann 2016). Hence, transient boredom may be a critical trait of the ambitious.

Each scale is based on different conceptions of boredom and therefore offers different results (Mercer-Lynn et al. 2013). While BSS associated boredom with "motor impulsivity, sensitivity to reward, gambling, and alcohol use and lower levels of neuroticism, experiential avoidance, and sensitivity to punishment" (p. 585), BPS associated boredom with "neuroticism, experiential avoidance, attentional and nonplanning impulsivity, anxiety, depression, dysphoria, and emotional eating" (p. 585). Currently, there is no one conclusive scale for measuring boredom. Both simple and complex/existential boredom are driven by anomie. The next chapter will describe boredom's historical birth in both Anglo and Russian society and will root its emotional experience within specific contexts, revealing its archetypes and cultural tropes.

Note

1 Many Russian words for boredom are commonly used by children.

2 Boredom's historical roots

Boredom is the threshold of great deeds.

Walter Benjamin 1927–1940[1]

Despite its extraordinary variety of diversions and resources, its frenzy for spectacles and its feverish pursuit of entertainment, AMERICA IS BORED. The abundance of efforts made in the United States to counter boredom have defeated themselves, and boredom has become the disease of our time.

Gooding (1976) Reader's Digest

In order to understand the emergence of boredom, we first need to elaborate on its historical and sociological context and perform an 'archeology' of its language. With the advent of modernity, a crisis of meaning arose in Western society which set the ground for the possibility of boredom. In order for society to maintain stability, its members must authentically believe in its tradition and in their specific social roles. With the advent of modernity, there was a breakdown of tradition followed by ubiquitous identity confusion. This set the foundational social organization for boredom. The hallmark event of modernity—the industrial revolution—created both a middle class and the idea of and time for leisure.

However, free unstructured leisure time revealed itself as inherently anomic; it lent itself to the possibility and spread of the novel emotion of boredom. In *The Conquest of Happiness*, the philosopher Bertrand Russell ([1930] 2013, p. 189) wrote: "To be able to fill leisure intelligently is the last product of civilization". In line with this sentiment, McDonough (2017) emphasizes that leisure time became empty and yet, maintained subjectivity and individuality. With modernity, free time and boredom democratized. We now have free time but are unsure of how to meaningfully experience it. With surplus free time, we realize our failure of character and will. Haladyn (2015, p. 109) explains boredom in relation to will: "boredom is not just a superficial inconvenience of lived existence but rather functions as an acknowledgement of the failure of the will to create meaning in a merely subjective world". This current-day ubiquitous problem entered vogue in the 18th and 19th centuries in Anglo and Russian society as the dominant theme in its respective literary traditions.

Historical Archetypes

Riesman's ([1950] 2001) archetype of the tradition-directed person can help us invoke a formerly common and currently rare personality-type to better understand the modern human. The tradition-directed person was an extension of a currently declining and potentially deceased, stable social order which was a virtually unchanging and upheld by conformist membership in a clan or caste, which determined relationships amongst its members. Prior to modernity, tradition thrived with limited innovation and 'generation effects' of modification. Rigid social etiquette was internalized via childhood socialization and maintained through ritual and religion (Riesman [1950] 2001).

As tradition reigned and maintained characterological obedience, there was minimal choice, as well as minimal emphasis on new solutions, activism for change, or the possibility for individualistic character. Riesman ([1950] 2001, p. 15) emphasizes: "individuality of character need not be highly developed to meet prescriptions that are objectified in ritual and etiquette". The tradition-directed person conceives himself as an essential component of the group and neither considers himself an individual nor the possibility of separate and personal goals.

Prior to modernity, tradition reigned and most people, atoms composing society, were tradition-oriented. Even 'mis-fits' were absorbed as shamans and monastics (Riesman ([1950] 2001). And even orders saturated with sadism and misery maintained conformism, stability and discouraged change. People self-censored their behavior for fear of shame. Prior to modernity, social change and progress were not esteemed values. Dependence on kin, hierarchy, adjustment, and continuation were upheld and deemed unshakeable. With modernity and its essential qualities of open and flexible social order, regular innovation, and constant novelty, society transitioned to inner and other-directedness.

Essentialism versus constructivism

Ontologically, this research serves as a powerful case against essentialism and in support of constructivism vis-à-vis illustrating the polarized tropes of boredom in Anglo and Russian society. I establish that boredom is a historical phenomenon, which emerged in modernity with different cultural expressions. This case stands in opposition to the popular narrative of the democratization of one type of boredom as a common experience open to all citizens of modernity and offers evidence for the multitude and diverse 'boredoms' of two distinct societies. It explains the diverging boredoms with variable culturally-specific 'anomies'. I demonstrate that different types of anomie cause different constructions of boredom.

The essentialist camp views 'boredom' as inherent to humanity and unhistorical, stating that all people throughout time and across space have experienced boredom. Proponents of this view state that the experience of boredom has always existed while its language has changed. Neologisms of boredom are arbitrary as all words from acedia to 'boredom' refer to the same phenomenon. Boredom's cause does not warrant investigation as it is a universal human experience. The Pulitzer Prize winning novelist Saul Bellow ([1975] 2008), Healy

([1927] 1984), Henry (2013), Phillips (1993), and Toohey (2011) are the main proponents of this view. Healy (1984) posits that boredom is a normal human mood. Saul Bellow (2008, p. 199) states that it is a variation on ancient states such as acedia. Phillips (1993) implies that boredom is inherent to human nature, and is both a common childhood experience and a common adult fear. He posits that boredom is a mood that "negates the possibility of explanation…certainly not pathological but nevertheless somehow unacceptable" (p. 71). Henry (2013) frames boredom as an affective state of unrealized potential inherent to human nature that arises in its own right from no external cause. Phillips (1993, p. 68), in his psychoanalytic chapter on the boredom of childhood, implies that it is a common childhood experience: "Every adult remembers … the great ennui of childhood, and every child's life is punctuated by spells of boredom". He implies that boredom is universal throughout humanity. In line with Phillips (1993), Toohey (2011) postulates that boredom is a common human emotion of mild disgust experienced in ordinary life from childhood throughout the lifespan. Hence, Toohey views boredom as an important defense mechanism inherent to humanity.

Conversely, Simmel ([1903] 1969), Betty Friedan ([1963] 2013), Spacks (1995), Goodstein (2005), and Johnsen (2016) are of the historical constructivist camp. Their research makes sociological and historical claims, calling boredom a modern phenomenon of 'lived meaninglessness'. They posit that emotional experience is culturally-bound and that boredom did not exist until the eighteenth century and has not spread to most of the world. Emotional experience is culturally-specific, an extension of social order, and is symptomatic of cultural maladjustment. Betty Friedan's *Feminine Mystique* (1963, p. 393) describes the boredom of American housewives stuck in the domesticity of "the comfortable concentration camp". She diagnoses the environment and housewife role as inducing boredom. Spacks (1995) writes that boredom arose during modernity,[2] along with the related experience of leisure which allowed life to be "interesting, thrilling, or exciting" (p. 10). She emphasizes that emotions are a package deal and that before the birth of boredom, its sister experiences of interest, thrill, and excitement also did not exist; boredom cannot exist without its polarities. She writes on the common belief that boredom is caused by stagnation and lack of stimulation, and that progress would make life more stimulating and banish boredom. She posits that, experientially, boredom is driven by poor focus, as we cannot be interested in something unless we pay attention and fully experience it. This study will advance Spacks' view of the historical emergence and social causes of boredom.

In Russian society, the cultural war between Slavophilism and Westernism serves as a supporting case for the social construction of boredom. During the 18th and 19th centuries, Russia was experiencing fast-paced modernization, driven by Western influence and a desire on behalf of the Tsars and aristocracy to keep up with their European neighbors. Before this period, there was no record or references to boredom. With the debut of Peter the Great's modernization efforts, Russia began importing ideas, standards, and language from Western Europe, including language for boredom. In fact, one of the first words for boredom (*skuka*) was first published and defined in Russian in 1704

(Shaposhnikov 2010). Critically, the importation of Western European values and concepts led to Russians demoting their own values and Russianness. This rejection had two major consequences. First, it led to mass confusion and malaise and, as relevant to this study, proliferated the experience of boredom. As Russians judged their traditions inferior and retrograde, they rejected the old and deemed it meaningless. There are several prominent examples. Duels which were formerly led to re-establish honor, began to be driven by drunken aimlessness and the need to pass time. While marriage, formerly driven by family arrangement, with deconstructed conventional morality, became a matter of personal attraction, connection, and romantic love—deeming arranged platonic marriage boring and meaningless and considering love confusing and unpredictable (Anna Karenina serves as the reified archetype of this value shift).

Second, modernity and the opening up of society, drove Slavophilism which aimed to revive authentic Russian values and block the spread of Western ideas. Slavophilism is a philosophical, religious, and political movement beginning in the 1830s which believes in reviving Russian ethnic tradition and uses its values as a model for Russian progress. They see 'the West' as an anti-model and write that Russia's degeneration, alienation, and boredom is due to looking West and importing Western ideas. They wrote that Russia should develop along its own values and should continue to hold them as sacred models for contemporary development and progress (Kireevskii, Jakim, & Khomiakov. 1998). Slavophilism began collaterally with Russia's literary tradition which also focused on problems of alienation, degeneration, and boredom for the first time. Alexander Pushkin and Ivan Turgenev are the most notable examples of classic writers who first recorded Russians' contemporary strivings and the new experience of the 'superfluous man', an archetype coined in Russian literature to describe existential non-belonging and its characteristic tropes of boredom.

Table 2.1 Literary causes of boredom

←***Anglo literature***—Affluence and not having to work—Difficulty filling one's leisure time/idleness—Foolishness—Distraction—Framed as a status symbol—Creative pursuit/change of circumstances—***Russian literature***→

Table 2.2 Literary reactions to boredom

←***Rejects/denies experience***—Suicide—Avoidance—Distraction—Framed as a status symbol (Conspicuous boredom)—Creative pursuit/change of circumstances—***Celebrates experience***→

Table 2.3 Narrative continuum

←***Explicit rejection/denial*** Tyutchev—Tolstoy—Pushkin—Lermontov—Orwell—Dickens—Disraeli (Silver Spoon Genre) ***Reframing/celebrating***→

Russian writers and thinkers primarily belong to the 'constructivist' camp positing that boredom is circumstantial and generational. Boredom is portrayed as a 'modern' and 'class act', limited to the 'new generation' and to the leisure class of aristocrats and the affluent. Elders and older generations are romanticized in the specific, national and religious, 'Slavophile' language of being piously connected to Russia, its heritage, and traditions. They are remembered as grounded in their Orthodox faith and content with traditional ways. Modern Russians are framed as being sponges, absorbing the bad influences of Western Europe, including its tendencies to empty leisure time and its infamous spectrum of emotional diseases—including boredom. Russian literature clearly establishes boredom as a common modern experience of disconnection from Russian tradition and connects it with the importation of European ideas, as demonstrated throughout this book.

Anglo society

> The worlds a game; Save that the puppets pull at their own strings.... There's little left but to be bored or bore.
>
> Byron (1824), Don Juan

Although prior scholars dated the English etymology of boredom to the 18th century (Goodstein 2005, Healy 1984, Spacks 1995), I discovered that Robert Burton ([1621] 2017, p. cii) used "bored" in his famous *The Anatomy of Melancholy*: "He had need to be bored, and so did all his fellows, as wise as they would seem to be", where boredom is attributed to foolishness. However, the word ('to bore')[3] was not defined in dictionaries until 1778: "a thing that causes ennui or annoyance". Although 'to bore' and its grammatical variants were neologisms without linguistic or cultural precedent, scholars have not explained the need for this new word (Healy 1984). Pezze and Salzani (2009, p. 12) emphasize: "Boredom was invented when and because a new experience demanded a new vocabulary and new forms of expression". From 1778, with its rendering in dictionaries, it entered the English lexicon. Healy (1984) writes:

> [it] was untraceable with any certainty to a word of previous formation.... The new term was evidently needed to give focused expression to a malaise that had increased in such degree, incidence, and reflective awareness, that it now called for a new, exact, vernacular form to replace or to substitute for the alien and only narrowly available ennui, and the always somewhat literary 'spleen', both of which were within a relatively short time displaced by the newcomer. (p. 24)

Before the neologism 'boredom' came into being, the French variant of 'ennui' was used. In 1667, as referenced by Klapp (1986, p. 24), the Oxford English Dictionary published a letter by a writer complaining that the English language does not have an equivalent for the French ennui. Its variants soon came into use, as did its literary prominence. The noun 'bore' initially appeared in the late eighteenth century and the noun 'boredom' was first used in the nineteenth century (Pezze & Salzani 2009).

Boredom's first known private appearance dates to 1768 in a letter written by the Earl of Carlisle describing French visitors as boring (Spacks 1995. In English literature, Lord Byron's poem *Childe Harold's Pilgrimage* ([1812] 2009), Catherine Gore's *Romances of Real Life* ([1829] 2017), Edgar Allen Poe's short story *Literary Life of Thingum Bob, Esq* ([1844] 2013) were three of the first works to use the word 'boredom'. Poe writes: "We could inflict no punishment so severe, and we would inflict it, but for the boredom which we should cause our readers in so doing" (Poe 2013, p. 33). During the 1840s, 'borism' was a newly coined and popularly used term; although this form did not survive, it suggests the spread of a new experience (Healy 1984).

In 1852, Charles Dickens followed, using the word 'boredom' in the first 12 chapters of the novel *Bleak House*, in which Lady Dedlock is described as bored to death until she actually dies. Although she finds boredom unbearable and in one scene faints from it, her boredom defines her high status: it is both of the existential and conspicuous variety. Gardiner and Haladyn (2017, pp. 5–6) write: "In Bleak House the word 'bored' designates the failure of the individual to generate consistent and lasting meaning within modern culture, to keep oneself occupied, an experience that feels like a mental and emotional death". Hence, from early English literary portrayals of boredom, characters were described as having difficultly filling leisure time. This is a notable distinction between Anglo and Russian 'causes' of boredom:

Since then, English literature has widely written on boredom, from George Eliot's *Daniel Deronda* ([1876] 1996) to entire genres such as contemporary Australian 'Grunge Lit'. Such literature describes and exposes the varieties of boredom: from an avoided aberration to a symbol of prestige.

Importantly, as displayed in the above charts, major characters of Russian literature, as few pro-active and productive options exist in their society, succumb to rejecting and denying their experience, and, occasionally, tragically ending in suicide. These cases are discussed below. Conversely, major characters of English literature often pro-actively reframe their experience as a status symbol (conspicuous boredom). Importantly, no characters represented in classic literature are successful in transcending their boredom entirely and transmuting it into enjoyable creative and productive activity.

Synonyms

Although boredom has synonyms which predate its etymology, most were solely referenced in the religious context and carried religious connotations; these have fallen out of use. Synonyms of boredom include sloth, acedia, anhedonia, and ennui. Sloth refers to indifference and affectlessness and is one of the seven deadly sins recorded by the Christian monk Evagrius Ponticus in the 4th century (Healy 1984). *Acedia* is a term from Christianity also dating to the early 4th century originally meaning spiritual or mental sloth or laziness, and later acquiring the connotations of apathy, boredom, laziness, and rejection of that which is spiritually good (Healy 1984). Originally, this term developed from one of the seven deadly sins or capital vices[4], sloth, and it continues to carry religious connotations and the judgment of moral insufficiency. *Acedia* differs from boredom in that it refers to spiritual laziness and is considered a Christian sin and an individual ethical failure. Hence, as contemporary boredom lacks religious and spiritual connotation and moral judgement, *acedia* is not an accurate synonym of boredom. Importantly, it disappeared from common use starting from 14th century, and scholars such as Robert Burton no longer employed the term (Healy 1984).

Two synonyms emerged after the etymology of 'boredom', and their use is limited to either specialized fields or is rare. Anhedonia is a term that dates to 1896 (Di Giannantonio & Martinotti 2012), from psychiatry, describing a common symptom of depression: the inability to feel pleasure from activities usually found enjoyable such as music, social interaction (known as social anhedonia), hobbies, sex (known as sexual anhedonia), food, or a general desire to engage in activities (known as motivational anhedonia). Anhedonia is an accurate synonym of boredom as they both share a similarity of the inability to experience enjoyment. Ennui was first used in 1660 and refers to boredom, listlessness, weariness, or discontent resulting from satiety or lack of interest. Ennui expanded to refer to depression, hopelessness, and a sense of life's meaninglessness. Unlike 'boredom' which is in common and frequent usage, ennui's use is quite rare. The latter is an experience particular to adulthood, and carries connotations of being, 'elite', 'aristocratic', sophisticated, and snobby. Its meaning overlaps with the conspicuous variety of boredom in that it may involve posturing and is seen as fashionable.

Although the etymology of boredom is clearly identified, the cause of the neologism is less known. There are two main ways of conceptualizing the birth of boredom:

1   Essentialists posit that boredom is an inherently human and timeless experience in all society. Proponents of this view state that the experience of boredom has always existed while its language has changed (Healy [1927] 1984; Phillips 1993; Toohey 2011). Neologisms of boredom are arbitrary as all words from acedia to 'boredom' refer to the same phenomenon. Boredom's cause does not warrant investigation as it is a universal human experience.

2   Constructivist scholars posit that boredom is historically and culturally bound. Proponents of this view state that boredom, especially existential or complex boredom, is a modern emotional experience which arose in the 18th century. Most write that the industrial revolution led to boredom by developing two classes of people: factory workers and an affluent leisure class. The former suffered from the 'simple boredom' of mindless repetition while the latter suffered from the 'existential boredom' of struggling to fill their leisure time and to find meaning in their lives. As evidence, they cite the explicit use of 'boredom' in dictionaries and literature.

The scientific study of boredom: from biological to sociological epistemology

Although Russian dictionaries and literature have referenced boredom since 1704 and English ones since 1778, its scientific study began in the 1840s with the investigation of its physiological characteristics (ex. Helmholz and Mary ran boredom studies) (Gardiner and Haladyn 2017). British meteorologist, statistician, and anthropologist Francis Galton, who came to be considered the father of boredom studies, continued its investigation in 1885 and 1889 with the examination of fidgeting and mental fatigue in the classroom. Gardiner, a fellow in the British Royal Society and the cousin of Charles Darwin, further influenced Galton's methodology. In the 1800s, in line with the positivist tradition, science generally viewed boredom, along with other mental states such as suicidality—before Durkheim's famous study, through the lens of biology and through the mechanics of the body (Gardiner and Haladyn 2017). Galton was the first scientist to think of boredom in terms of context, appreciating it as a mental state separate from the body. However, he evaluated boredom statistically in terms of external cues such as fidgeting and aimed to quantify the experience. He was more focused on quantification than on developing a full accurate definition and understanding of its causes.

Schopenhauer's epistemology

Schopenhauer was one of the first philosophers to notice and write on boredom which he conceived as a longing without an object, a sensation and evidence of the worthlessness of existence (Schopenhauer [1851] 1973, pp. 53–54). Schopenhauer insisted that if life was inherently meaningful or had a positive value, boredom wouldn't exist. Those afflicted, have to struggle against the condition. Importantly, his view was constructivist, positing that boredom is not essential to human nature and extends from intelligence and class (Schopenhauer [1818] 1966). He insisted that knowledge and intelligence increase one's capacity for pain, including boredom. Geniuses and the affluent are most prone to boredom. According to Schopenhauer, animals as well as the poor experience 'want' and pain but not boredom. Describing the wealthy, Schopenhauer writes (2010):

> for whom their very wealth now becomes a punishment by delivering them into the hands of tormenting boredom. To escape from this, they now rush about in all directions and travel, here, there, and everywhere. No sooner do they arrive at a place than they anxiously inquire about its amusements and clubs, just does as a poor man about its sources of assistance. (p. 5)

Intelligent people can relieve boredom by aesthetic absorption in art and music and by invoking mystical states. Schopenhauer concludes that boredom and death are closely-knit driving both suicide and homicide ([1851] 1973, p. 43).

Schopenhauer's worldview also overlap's with Durkheim's explanatory concept of anomie. Referencing anomie, Mestrovic (1993, p. xiii) writes: "these religious and traditional dimensions also meshed, again, with the popularity of

Schopenhauer's own notion of the infinitely striving will that makes the enlightened person suffer more, not less, than his or her ancestors". Schopenhauer's class-based formulation overlaps with Durkheim's assessment that poverty and limiting opportunity protects against suicide. Both posited that the class that Marx dismissed as bourgeoisie was more prone to psychological suffering. Hence, the torment of those struggling to survive is different from the suffering of boredom.

More recently, boredom's epistemological assumptions have been driven by social science and social structure-based models. Its research is focused on understanding the interplay between environment, such as cultural and parenting practices, and the mind. It focuses on how certain environmental experiences, such as the basic experience of waiting in line or the complex experience of living in an anomic society, trigger the emotion of boredom. As discussed in the introduction, the majority of research endorses anti-essentialism and the social constructivist model of ontology, as the word and concept only recently emerged and became part and parcel of modern Western Civilization. Although the novel and contemporaneous nature of boredom has been established, there remains no well-trodden path or clear direction for its investigation. There is no consensus regarding its definition or sociological causality. Without a clear precedent, its inherited legacy allows sociologists to easily chart novel discovery in terms of definition, history, causality, and ethnography, deeming its study terra incognita and refreshingly open.

Boredom and The American Psychological Association

The American Psychological Association (APA) has long conceived boredom and its symptomology, such as lack of focus and attention, not as a cultural or societal issue, but as an extension of a 'chemical imbalance' in the brain. Gardiner and Haladyn (2017, p. 32) have gone so far as to argue that "psychologists continue to pathologise non-conformity, labelling children ADHD and treating problems of meaning as symptoms of neurochemical imbalance" for the purposes of a bio-political agenda. As one out of dive children are currently taking ADD/ADHD medication and as such medications are part of a multi-billion dollar industry which feeds on a constant flow of new consumers (Gaviria 2001), their point is valid. Hence, the disciplines of psychology and psychiatry have encouraged us to conceive boredom as a symptom of biological mental illness treated with psychopharmacology, instead of a common emotion worth appreciating and appropriating to fuel our creative pursuits. In line with this and Gooding's (1976) observation quoted at the top of this chapter, it is important to consider to what degree every psychiatric medication is treating boredom, and to apply that information for social restructuring for boredom-prevention.

Russian society

> It's a new fashion they have invented, being bored; in the old days no one was bored.
>
> Nikolai Gogol ([1842] 2003), Dead Souls

Of course boredom may lead you to anything. It is boredom that sets one sticking gold pins into people.

Dostoyevsky 1864, Notes from the Underground

I found life so boring it drove me mad.

Dostoyevsky 1872, Demons

Boredom: The Desire for Desires

Tolstoy (2013)

Unlike English, which offers one word for 'boredom', Russian has at least four commonly used equivalents which may speak to the particularly complex emotional experience of Russian society, cultural bias towards emotional introspection and communication, and to the precision of its language. In fact, Russian society may offer emotional experiences distinct from its Anglo counterpart. Its synonyms of boredom capture its cause or the 'why' of the complex emotional experience. In Russian, all the words for boredom express its cause and consequences; examples follow.

In Russian, the term boredom can be rendered as *skuka* [скука], *tomleniye* [тёмление], *khandra* [Хандра], and *toska* [toска]. *Skuka* was first defined in Russian dictionaries in 1704 and means cramped, annoyed, bothered, or to be placed in a difficult situation, melancholy from a lack of interest in one's surroundings, and missing fun or entertainment (Shaposhnikov 2010). Mead, Gorer, and Rickman (2001) write "skuka corresponds in some ways to boredom … a feeling of loneliness and uselessness" (p. 104). Green (2014, p. 68) writes: "Skuka has connotations of anguish which are absent from its English counterpart". One who experiences skuka is aware of some void but is unable to identify it. Such a state can result from having unorganized free time or not knowing 'what to do with oneself'. Children often use *skuka* when referring to their common boredom of not knowing what to do next. As rendered by the famous poet Mikhail Lermontov (1830; as referenced in Morrissey 2007), *skuka* can also be driven-by a spiritual crisis of alienation from the world. Lermontov writes: "I am bored [*skuchno*] and sad, and there in no one to whom I can give my hand in the moment of my spiritual adversity". Connoting Riesman's study ([1950] 2001), *skuka* may also refer to the reified experience of being at a crowded party yet feeling deeply lonely. Such an experience is suggested by the refrain: "Water, water, everywhere, Nor any drop to drink" from *The Rime of the Ancyent Marinere* ([1798] 2017) by Coleridge.

Skuka remains in common usage in contemporary Russian. Morrissey (2007, p. 160) writes: "The Russian word for boredom is skuka" and as boredom, *skuka seems to possess the dual meaning of simple and existential boredom.* Hence, *skuka* and Anglo definitions of boredom seem to have overlapping and synonymous meanings (Mead, Gorer, & Rickman 2001). To protect and heal oneself from *skuka*, Russian literature suggests avoiding the vice of idleness and keeping busy, working, moderation in amusement and luxury [excessive comfort], cultivating virtue, and living for others (Morrissey 2007).

Importantly, *skuka* made its debut under Peter the Great's reign during his modernization project. His reforms included a new Cyrillic script and approximately 1,000, mostly Latin-derived, neologisms (Cracraft 2004, p. 68), borrowed from Western Europe; some became standard Russian while many eventually became obsolete (Cracraft 2004. Cracraft writes:

> the number of new words that were fixed in Russian during the thirty or so years of Peter's active reign … and of Russian derivations that were quickly formed from these words (usually adjectives, verbs, or adverbs formed from new nouns) was entirely unprecedented in Russia or, very likely anywhere else in so short a time. When the semantic range of all these neologisms is considered, the breadth of subjects and meanings involved, this lexical influx alone is nothing short of revolutionary. (p. 105)

Hence, a new political reality focused on adopting Western values of scientific, infrastructural, and humanitarian progress led to the adoption and creation of approximately 1,000 new words, including boredom or *skuka*. Although circumstantial evidence suggests that this word was imported from Western Europe, no record of such a borrowing exists.

Tomleniye was first used in the early 19th century and means testing vexation, inconsolable languor, or painful yearning. *Tomleniye* can occur from almost any experience: waiting, uncertainty, laziness, idleness, satiety, and from an inability to set goals. *Tomleniye* often arises during pauses, in between goals, or in states of hiatus. When we complete a major life goal, such as finishing our education, marrying, or buying a home, and have yet to set new goals, we risk *tomleniye*. While Alexander Pushkin (1821[5]), Nikolai Gogol (1831[6]), and Anton Chekhov (1896)[7] wrote of *tomleniye* in the 19th century, it was formally defined, after its entrance into literature in 1847 in the Academic Dictionary. The poet Fyodor Tyutchev personally felt *tomleniye* when he yearned for returning abroad but was forced to remain in Saint Petersburg. Tyutchev, famously, experienced such *tomleniye* that he was willing to kill and risk dying for its resolution. Having learned that the punishment for winning a duel (by inflicting a deadly shot to one's rival) is punished by being sent abroad, he made plans to duel. It is often used in the context of "she misses someone and is unable to enjoy her current experience" [Ona tomitsya]. As *tomleniye* refers to a painful yearning for something to happen, its meaning overlaps with Anglo definitions of boredom.

Khandra was first used in the 19th century and refers to a boredom characterized by longing, melancholy "tinged with idleness" (Plamper 2015, p. 293), and irritability (Pushkin 2009). It captures the experience of those who aren't sure what they want to do and whom they want to see, as nothing and no one excites them. It refers to a bored restlessness, irritability, and a rejection of the present and its options. Dobrenko and Naiman (2011) write:

> At the beginning of the 19th century, boredom was thought to be an aristocratic illness. A bored visage entered the code of social behavior as a sign of

refinement and nobility.... The satiated man, master of everything and acquainted with all, could not help but be bored. (p. 283)

In line with this rendering, Grant (2009, p. 102) defines *khandra* as "cultivated melancholy". Pushkin's ([1825–1832] 2009) *Eugene Onegin* suffers from a deep *khandra* which blocks him from enjoying everything from celebrations to romance. And yet, we know that he has *khandra*, and not depression, because he clearly maintains his self-confidence.[8] The composer Tchaikovsky famously suffered from *khandra*, which in a letter to his sister, he attributed to his "circumstances as a bachelor ... to the complete absence of selflessness in my life.... [I] care only about myself.... This is very convenient, of course, but dry, deadly, narrow" (Gasparov 2008, p. 71). Tchaikovsky was convinced that his *khandra* was driven-by the egocentrism of being a superfluous man in his personal life. This archetype of the 'superfluous man' is 'the' character of Russian literature (Chances 1978).

Toska was first used in the 19th century and refers to boredom punctuated by vague restlessness and yearning, often, without a specific cause. The famous Russian author Vladimir Nabokov (as referenced by Hitesh 2013) elaborates:

No single word in English renders all the shades of toska. At its deepest and most painful, it is a sensation of great spiritual anguish, often without any specific cause. At less morbid levels it is a dull ache of the soul, a longing with nothing to long for; a sick pining, a vague restlessness, mental throes, yearning. In particular cases it may be the desire for somebody of something specific, nostalgia, love-sickness, at the lowest level it grades to ennui, boredom. (p. xiii)

Its synonyms are melancholy, sadness, depression, boredom, ennui, weariness, nostalgia, yearning, anguish, and agony. *Toska* is commonly used in contemporary Russian to describe the restless boredom of living in the countryside and the yearning for someone or something such as one's homeland and the collateral inability to find meaning in one's current circumstances (Wierzbicka 1992). It has the same root as *toschii* (emaciated) and signals spiritual emptiness which longs to be filled. Wierzbicka (1992, p. 171) writes: "Toska implies the absence and the inaccessibility of something good". Toska's meaning overlaps with Anglo definitions of boredom.

Many have wondered why Russian has more words for boredom than English. Wierzbicka (1992) emphasizes that 'boredom', especially captured in the word 'toska' is a major theme in Russian identity and self-image. Additionally, Russian culture places a "tremendous stress on emotions and on their free expression", and Russian language offers a "wealth of linguistic devices for signaling emotions and shades of emotions" (p. 395). Importantly, unlike Anglo culture which stresses logic and rational thinking and views uninhibited emotions with suspicion and embarrassment, some prominent currents in Russian culture stress the limits of logic and encourage irrationality and emotional expression, seeing emotional expression as "one of the main functions of human speech" (Wierzbicka 1992,

p. 403). In line with this, Russians tend to be labile, easily expressing their emotional experience and giving into their emotions. Emotions that may be viewed as inappropriately intense and a sign of dysregulation in the Anglo context, including within its psychiatry framework, are considered acceptable and normative within the Russian context.

Russian culture, influenced by the Russian Orthodox tradition which stresses the emotional nature of religious experience, as well as by the self-consciously sentimentalist literary and anti-Enlightenment 'irrationalist' philosophical traditions, encourages the passive surrender to emotional experience. Wierzbicka (1992, p. 401) emphasizes: "Unlike English, Russian is extremely rich in 'active' emotional verbs...most (though not all) Russian emotional verbs are reflexive verbs, formed with the suffix –sja 'self'", implying that the emotions are self-induced versus externally-induced. For example, in English we tend to say 'I am glad or angry' while in Russian we tend to say 'I rejoice or fume'. Although Anglo culture is known for its individualism, psychological verbiage, and introspection, Russian offers more words for emotional experience and encourages raw emotional expression. Wierzbicka (1992) writes:

> The marginality of verbs of emotion in the English language reflects this cultural difference ... if one compares English with Russian, it is Russian which emerges as much more focused on emotions and much richer in both lexical and grammatical resources for differentiating emotions. (p. 403)

Russian offers emotions as 'passive-experiential' and encourages one to see oneself as a passive experiencer (as lived or daily experience) and to express oneself as such.

Many of the most famous authors of Russian literature have used the language, concept, and theme of boredom. In most of Russian literature, boredom leads to personal hedonism and to the downfall of the character and his close ones. Alexander Pushkin's main character of *Eugene Onegin* suffers from a deep sense of being a 'superfluous man' who does not fit into society's norms and feels unneeded. As a result, Onegin suffers from existential boredom (existential forms of *skuka* and *toska*), carelessness, cynicism, and a lack of empathy for others. Onegin responds by disregarding social values, gambling, drinking, and by engaging in romantic drama and duels to fill his time. The story opens with Onegin complaining about caring for his sick uncle who will soon bequeath him his manor: "But God, what deadly boredom, brothers, To tend a sick man night and day" (Pushkin [1825–1832] 2009, p. 5). Throughout the novel in verse, although Onegin's life consists of the ongoing entertainment of parties and concerts, his default state is one of grave boredom and disaffection. While in 1840, Mikhail Lermontov published the novel *A Hero of Our Time* in which the antihero Pechorin experiences *skuka*, emptiness, and indifference which lead him to indulge in hedonistic pleasures, eventually resulting in his and his close ones' downfall.

Depictions of boredom are ubiquitous in Russian literature. As *skuka*, *tomleniye*, and *toska* are synonymous with boredom, from now on, in most references, I will simply use the general term 'boredom' without specifying the particular Russian-equivalent. From 1855 to 1863, Alexander Afanasyev published a collection of fairy tales including *The Princess Who Never Smiled* about a princess who was apathetic and miserable, unaffected by consistent attempts to improve her mood. Although the cause of the princess's boredom was unclear, it was temporarily relieved by humor. In 1888, Chekhov (2019) published the story "Lights" focused on the complexity of *skuka* as a negative generational experience, as an influence one could impose on others, as an experience one was powerless against, and vodka as an attempted antidote. On boredom as a negative generational experience, he comments ([1888] 2011[9]):

> Our generation has carried this dilettantism, this playing with serious ideas into science, into literature, into politics, and into everything which it is not too lazy to go into, and with its dilettantism has introduced, too, its coldness, its boredom, and its one-sidedness and, as it seems to me, it has already succeeded in developing in the masses a new hitherto non-existent attitude to serious ideas.

The narrator is disappointed in his generation for easily succumbing to boredom and dilettantism, and lazily 'playing with serious ideas' instead of applying themselves in systematic study.

The following year Chekhov published a short story titled *The Lady with the Dog* ([1899] 2016) which depicts an affair between a bored married woman and a Russian banker. Although she feels morally righteous and emphasizes her guilt about infidelity, her boredom is so intolerable that she succumbs to infidelity. They fall in love with each other and only experience happiness when together, while when separated, both suffer from a deep longing for one another, depression, and boredom.

Leo Tolstoy's *Anna Karenina* ([1873–1877] 2002) serves an archetypal example of boredom. It follows the tragic extramarital love affair of Anna, a married woman, with, an affluent army officer, Count Vronsky. She feels miserable in her platonic and passionless marriage and, for 19th century Imperial Russia, commits an act of personal authenticity and rebellion by openly abandoning her husband and son for her lover. The consequences are tragic and the novel ends in her suicide, as mentioned previously. Inadvertently, they experience anomic boredom starting after they elope to Italy and for the remainder of the novel. Their boredom is in the 'Russian style' in which both Anna and Vronsky have clearly self-defined identities (Riesman's ([1950] 2001) inner-directed type), yet their new Italian home and its people are unfamiliar, and they struggle relating to them, cultivating friendship, and in amusing themselves. They are unable to develop a healthy social identity vis-à-vis social adjustment. Hence, in Italy they experience the anomie of changing place which leads to boredom—especially for Vronsky, who finds himself restless.

When they attempt to re-establish themselves in Russian high society, Vronsky is accepted and allowed freedom of movement while Anna is shunned and snubbed, leaving her isolated and bored. Anna is alienated from her own class and left existentially homeless: she clearly self-identifies as a member of Russian society and although her identity is unshakable, due to social rejection, she is unable to adjust and to feel at home in society, leaving her painfully and senselessly lost in anomic boredom. She wants to live in the world of society while rejecting its principles, which proves impossible.

Anna Karenina's story ([1873–1877] 2002) is one of displacement and non-belonging; she marries a man she loves platonically and does not want to belong to, falls passionately for another with whom she can never have a real home, and resides in a society which ostracizes the 'real her' under any circumstances (Part 5; Part 7). And so, instead of living out her life in existential boredom, she succumbs to suicide (Part 7). Patterson (1995) describes the relationship between identity and place in Russian literature:

> To take on an identity, then, is to take up a residence, to establish a home where one may dwell rather than take to a fortress where we merely survive, it is to have a place and a presence from which one human being may step before the face of another and declare, "Here I am". Since dwelling is tied to such a capacity for response, the linkage to a dwelling place is determined by a linkage between word and meaning, between self and other. (pp. x–xi)

Applying Patterson's framework to *Anna Karenina*, we can imagine that she was exiled and found herself in the state of anomic homelessness. Initially, this leads to chronic maladjustment and eventually to her last act of suicide. Suicide is an important and common cultural act in then Russian society. Paperno (1997) explains:

> [i]t was only in the 1860s, during the Great Reforms, which created many new public institutions (organs of the press, open courts, statistical bureaus), that suicide became an object of vigorous discussions in science, law, fiction, and above all, the periodical press. Between the 1860s and the 1880s, Russia was believed to have experienced an 'epidemic of suicides', which left volu-minous records. A time of radical change is Russian society, coincidental with an intellectual revolution—the rise of positivism—the reform era created a cultural context in which suicide acquired an array of meanings and became a symbol of the age. (p. 3)

Boredom and suicide coincide throughout Russian literature. I would like to underline that besides for boredom, anomie triggers a spectrum of related emo-tional dis-eases including, as Durkheim established, the final attempt of ending one's suffering: suicide. This is reflected in Russian literature: while some characters suffer ongoing existential boredom, others chose to end their life.

The concept of the superfluous man

Russian literature attributes boredom to being a product of a leisure class that requires little of the individual, which caused him to feel 'superfluous' in society

(Chances 1978). As the 'superfluous man' is an extra in society, he rejects it, and suffers from the existential crisis of finding himself and of relating to his context. This concept is unique to Russian literature and highlights a critical distinction between boredom depicted in Russian versus in English-language literature. The superfluous man suffers, not from the latter style of boredom during which one does not know one's purpose and as an extension of an unclear identity, struggles to occupy oneself, but from a clearly identified Russian style of boredom which results from chronic *social restraint* and *non-belonging*. This framing overlaps with Riesman's ([1950] 2001) concept of the inner-directed person. The Russian character knows himself well yet finds himself in a jarring mismatch with society, leaving him existentially homeless, in chronic anomie and subsequent boredom (Patterson 1995). Hence, unlike boredom in English-speaking discourse, boredom in Russian discourse is characterized by a clear sense of self-awareness, social restraint, 'homelessness', and alienation. *The bored Russian is hyper self-conscious of his unconventionality and is unable to reconcile the tension between himself and society*, leaving him generally passive and 'useless', in terms of social participation.

The Russian case clearly demonstrates that anomie is experienced in proportion to non-belonging. Anomie is the price for poor social fit (Riesman [1950] 2001). The lower the congruence between character and norms/expectations/task, the higher the subjective anomie. The recalcitrant suffer. Yet, their presence, cultural reification in literature, art, and politics, and the quantitative increase in such character may signal the ineffectuality and decay of traditional institutions. *The birth of the anomic character is a symptom of a cultural disease, a sign of a structural blind spot, and evidence of a leak in the symbolic typology of our world.* Our society no longer holds us, as it did, when traditional man reigned. Anomie is a sign of the virgin smoke of a raging forest fire. If noticed, understood, embraced, and treated, humanity has a chance of survival and rejuvenation as a conscious and deliberate community. If ignored, anomie and decay will proceed, as will its complementary processes of boring art and charismatic rule, and are explored in the following chapters.

Notes

1 *The Arcades Project* was published in segments between 1927 and 1940.
2 This is a similar argument to Philippe Aries' in *Centuries of Childhood: A Social History of Family Life* (1962) where he establishes the experience of childhood to be a modern experience (with the exception of children of monarchs and aristocrats).
3 It was defined in another tense.
4 Originally, there were eight deadly sins or capital vices. Evagrius Ponticus removed *acedia*, by which there remained seven deadly sins.
5 Pushkin and Kneller (2008).
6 Gogol and Kent (1985).
7 Chekhov and Garnett (2014).
8 Depression is characterized by low self-confidence/self-worth, a belief of unworthiness, and judging oneself as 'bad'.
9 Electronic copy; no page number listed.

3   Boredom as an art strategy

Boredom was until recently, one of the qualities an artist tried most to avoid. Yet today it appears that artists are deliberately trying to make their art boring.

Dick Higgins 1968

The public venerates boredom. For boredom is mysterious and profound. The listener is defenseless against boredom. Boredom subdues him.

Erik Satie[1]

On a basic level, art gives form to experience. Historically, art was a social institution teaching morals, inspiring people to be better, and expressing beauty in its purest form. It promoted the idea that art was the redemption of mankind, compensating for its moral failures. The Renaissance birthed this ethos which continued to characterize art until WWI. Its method was sensory stimulation through representation. Examples include every cultural icon from the Sistine Chapel and the symphonies of Bach and Beethoven to classical ballet. But this idea of art is now dead.

In the beginning stages of art's paradigm shift, its subject matter widened to include portrayals of boredom and its referent social arrangements. Upon viewing paintings such as *Waiting for the Times* (1831) by Benjamin Haydon, *The Marriage of Convenience* (1883) by Sir William Orchardson, or *When the Boats are Away* (1903) by Walter Langley, we may assume that Anglo depictions of boredom were a timeless and regular occurrence. However, this social affliction was in fact new and unexpected. Paintings depicting boredom reflected a new social reality in which boredom became a ubiquitous state. This novel phenomenon was generally seen as an experience of unclear or unpleasant waiting and disengagement. Such paintings rendered distant demeanors with faces turned away from the viewer, from each other, or completely concealed. The captured scenes themselves are quite dull. *Waiting for the Times* (1831) by Haydon captures an aristocratically-dressed man gazing at his companion who is reading the paper, consumed in his own experience with little regard for all else.

The Marriage of Convenience (1883) by Sir Orchardson invites us into a scene of an older man dining with his disconnected and displeased younger wife. With her look of outward blasé, she signals her disregard for him and for the dinner, and that she awaits the end of his companionship. There is an explicit withdrawal of emotional affect. Both subjects are objectified—their relations are reduced to a contractual agreement. *When the Boats are Away* (1903) by Langley offers us a slow glance at an older man (likely a fisherman) who is in a state of waiting for the boats to return, while he reads the paper and while his wife stands by holding a large basket with an absence of emotional affect. The scene presents little of interest. After boredom's novel introduction as an aesthetic subject matter, art underwent an unprecedented cataclysmic transformation with the coming of World War I, whereby its very style imported boredom for its own means.

This drastic turn severed ties with tradition and pre-WWI culture, and transformed into a new social institution oriented towards radical novelty, disdain for the audience, and scathing deconstruction of former aesthetic techniques and themes. New and old pre-war artists alike lost faith in the ideals of the Renaissance; they concluded that they had reached an exhaustion of form and would have no choice but to reconstruct the entire institution of art fueled by individualism and deconstruction. This new art became nihilistic, defacing traditional cultural icons such as the painting of the Mona Lisa with a mustache (Duchamp and Dali), displaying objects found by the side of the road (found art) and sharing ordinary objects such as trash, bodily fluids, toilets, refrigerator doors, and objects draped in textiles (junk and disposable art). It was meant to kill the pre-war artistic ethos. It used boredom as a strategy.

The pre-war art strove to be interesting and engaging. Conversely, the new birth child was so individualistically-focused, its drive for self-expression trumped everything else, including art's original purpose of conveying meaning to its audience. Where the old art aimed to express the beauty of the natural-order-of-things, the new art rejected this order but more importantly, it offered no cohesive philosophy of its own. The leftover void was filled with radical cries of self-expression, echoing the existential crisis of immediate post-WWI culture.

While techniques such as displaying simple objects democratized the production of art, they created huge cultural barriers to fully appreciating and understanding it. Examples of this include René Magritte's famous pipe painting with the caption 'this is not a pipe' ([1928–1929] 2019), collected menstruation blood (Martincic 2016), and the recent Maurizio Cattelan's $120,000-priced banana duct-taped to a wall (Morrissey 2019) which was eaten by a spectator. Ordinary people struggled to understand and appreciate the artistic reasoning behind declaring common objects as art. This novel institution has remained inherently elitist. The consequences of its elitism have resulted in the decline of art's status and popularity as a respectable social institution as well as mass illiteracy in art. In his famous treatise *The Dehumanization of Art*, Spanish philosopher Ortega y Gasset ([1925] 2019, p. 4) writes: "All modern art is unpopular, and it is so not accidentally and by chance, but essentially". This has reached a pinnacle where being an artist is socially taboo and an abhorrent career path according to most parents.

What is the purpose of boredom in art?

At first glance, the title of this chapter contradicts itself: why would artists create boring art? Invoking classical art connotes inspiring and evocative subject matter, being swayed by a deluge of powerful emotions, the incredible imagination and skill of artists, memorably beautiful form, or a historical moment forever preserved in a piece of art. Boredom and art do not seem to belong together.

That is until we consider art as a Durkheimian social institution, enacting strategies to accomplish its end goal. For modern art, boredom is such a strategy. *Modern art aims to resolve modernity's anomic crisis* of meaning by encouraging society to look inward and saturate personal experience with meaning. Unlike fine art in pre-modernity which was presented 'readymade', imbued with tradition and meaning, and offered a predictable, interesting, and stimulating experience, modern art mirrored the existential crisis of its social context: cries of alienation, maladjustment, disconnection, void, restlessness, and boredom. This new art spoke a progressive language and required deep audience engagement: it called for the resolution of dis-eased states by inviting subjective engagement and meaning-making. It offered to partake in cultural creation.

Modern art invoked a belief that subjectivity is truth and that truth is subjectivity, a Kierkegaard's reification of subjectivity (Kierkegaard [1846] 2009). It supposed that if you're made to feel bored, this state will trigger self-awareness of your unique observations that are only meaningful to you. Hence, if you're initially bored by a piece of art, and then find some aspect compelling, then your observation is subjectively significant. The creed of modern art is: 'Make art boring to help sustain individuality by encouraging the audience to find some aspect uniquely intriguing'. Its creed is in line with Kierkegaard's skepticism for objective truths. Driven by its humanistic ethos, modern art embodies boredom in visual, musical, dance, film, and theatrical form, serving as a call for subjective resolution through direct personal experience.

Another element of modern art is its 'counter-revolutionary' will to boredom, which offers the following viewing reactions: 1. passively remain bored and withdrawn; or 2. project yourself into the experience and craft meaning. Importantly, modern art is counter-revolutionary in that it implies: 1. current mainstream society is inadequate at providing experiential value and meaning; 2. modern values are insufficient and therefore, society has become boring; 3. boredom is a form of resistance to the commodity culture of 'readymade' (easily palatable) goods;[2] 4. boredom can be used to motivate change. In order for us to have a valuable experience, we must become our own experiential creators. Hence, modern art offers a social critique of contemporary society as anomic and suggests the possibility of resolution. With the unprecedented emergence of boredom, artists began rendering this new phenomenon in literature, theater, music lyrics, film, and in the visual arts as both a subject and deliberate audience effect.

This chapter will elaborate on the sociological causes of representations and the deliberate effects of boredom in painting, performance art, film, music, and dance, and comment on its temporal elements. With modernity, Western society acquires a crisis of meaning which permeates its social institutions, including art. In the contemporary zeitgeist, the purpose and logic of art has changed. Before, art was a high-status social institution focused on the sensory experience of form of the artist and of its audience; creating sensual enjoyment and stimulation.

Viewed from this perspective, attention span indicates quality: *the longer a piece can hold one's attention through sensory stimulation, the better the art.* For example, many have reported that they enjoy viewing the Mona Lisa almost indefinitely and return to it frequently.

On the other hand, modern art became subject to abundance and social critique, whereas many may see Marcel Duchamp's urinal once and lack a desire for repeat viewings. Barzun (2000) describes the novelty and entertainment-seeking of 16th century Italy:

> There is the ever-watchful boredom ready to pounce and destroy what has been too often tasted and touted. And when the really new is abundant, as it was in the romanticist period, it swamps the old by sheer weight of numbers. (p. 153)

For example, initially popular writers in the early 16th century, with the advent of a new generation of writers, lost their audience when readers became bored of the old literature. Barzun (2000) describes the 16th century's focus on musical harmony, by quoting Zarlino of Venice who wrote *Harmonic Principles* (1558):

> It would not be fitting to use a sad harmony and a slow rhythm with a gay text or a gay harmony and quick light-footed rhythm to a tragic matter full of tears. [The composer] must set each word to music in such a way that where it denotes hardness, cruelty, etc. the music must be similar to it, without offending. (p. 158)

During the Renaissance, harmony became such a critical tenet of the renaissance, that there was a major ideological debate between supporters of harmony (solo voice/melody) and supporters of polyphony (two or more voices/melodies performed simultaneously), from which harmony emerged. In polyphony, individual words are not heard as clearly as in harmonious melodies.

The piling up and collision of competing melodies can sound harsh with intolerable sounds (Barzun 2000). He describes the discovery of harmony:

> Out of this predicament comes the idea of composing vertically, that is, taking care about the collisions that occur between horizontal lines [the lines of sheet music]. This musical style bears the other obvious name of harmony. It offers the listener a melody visualized as being on top ... and having below a group of notes so chosen as not to shock the ear—or if they do, to do it in a passing way, quickly resolved into harmoniousness.... The seesaw in the history of music between harmony and polyphony is a characteristic instance of response to external demands, coupled with fatigue-and-boredom prompting change ... modern music [16th century] must be at once expressive and transparent; it must leave the words of the play intelligible. (p. 157–159)

The renaissance tradition emphasized the importance of music being harmoniously expressive and intelligible. This tradition contrasts greatly with modern composition, such as that of the *Aesthetic of Indifference* of John Cage, discussed later in this chapter.

During pre-modernity, mostly elites created and consumed art for their own sensory experience (as with religious painting and music, such an aesthetic experience had the purpose of invoking the divine). In order to fully 'appreciate' such art, you had to prepare by sensitizing yourself to certain auditory and visual stimuli. One is not born appreciating Da Vinci or Bach, but learns to appreciate fine art through a specific and sophisticated process of refinement.

This is not the case with modern art which can be created and understood by the masses. With modernity, art's purpose became ideological. Contemporary 'art' began spreading ideas and relayed social critique with the suggestion of resolution. This was likely the result of social institutions reflecting their zeitgeist.

The intended impact of modern art is personal and depends on one's capacity to actively and relationally participate. It relays its point (an idea) with instantaneous accessibility. Compared to its traditional predecessor, modern art is more about contemplative reflection and less about invoking tradition and sensory intensity. In modernity, art became democratized. With its mass production and consumption, its original 'purpose' lost its bearings and was replaced with a more practical and palpable purpose: spreading an idea or making a point.

The Anglo case

Dadaism, Surrealism, Minimalism, Pop Art, and American postwar avant-garde, known for creating the *Aesthetic of Indifference*, emerged as movements that did not want the everyday to be taken for granted and aimed to trigger introspection of the audience. These movements directly communicated with boredom. Haladyn (2015, pp. 131–132) posits that: "the will to boredom develops as an important artistic strategy within the culture of late-modernism and serves an active integration of boredom into the temporal and conceptual structuring of art as an experience". Modern art, through a 'will to boredom' aims to resolve the modern (anomic) crisis of meaning by encouraging its audience to glance anew at the boring and to find subjective meaning, illumination, and joy in the experience.

Specifically, two modern art movements, Dada and Surrealism, developed in an attempt to challenge the cultural status quo, strip art of high status and consumer capitalism of "ready-made relations and associations" (Haladyn 2015, p. 131) by presenting a banal aesthetic and encouraging the audience to re-envision their version of reality and to personalize experience. Gardiner and Haladyn (2017) writes:

> By the 1960s, visual art was no longer expected to be beautiful or skillfully rendered... Minimal art, one of American art's most influential but also most controversial developments, was based on large and simple forms and smooth, blank surfaces. If it was successful, the work's singular shape, scale and assertive presence in space elicited the beholder's interest. Yet, no modern development was more often accused of being 'boring'.... Now

recognized as the concluding chapter of modernism – modern art developing at the same time, in the mid-nineteenth century, as the modern affliction of boredom.... It was the ultimate step in the so-called modernist reduction, in which artworks became progressively simpler and stripped of detail, flatter and less illusionistic and more abstract ... **conservative critics like John Canaday of the New York Times accused Minimal art of meaninglessness**. (p. 67)

Such conservative critics found themselves bored by minimalism and accused modern art of being 'non-art'. They were correct in that, as discussed, the institution of art had transformed its purpose to the ideological. Its novel sentiment was: through the experience of personal meaning-making, you'll became equal to the artist. Modern Art democratized its production and the status of the artist, as art's value was framed as proportional to the spectator's experience.

Critically, Dada and Surrealism were reactive in nature and aimed to 'shake things up' and shock people out of their banal mainstream perspective. Haladyn writes: "these Dada events attempted to shock people's sensibilities in order to wake them from the complacent boredom of their everyday lives" (2015, p. 106). Case studies follow.

Man Ray was an American Dada and Surrealist who famously collaborated with Marcel Duchamp on a kinetic piece titled *Rotary Glass Plates* and helped found the Société Anonyme, Inc. which became the first collection of modern art in the US. In the vision of Dada, Man Ray directed some of the first Dadaist films (e.g. *Return to Reason* 1923, *Emak-Bakia* 1927, *The Starfish* 1928, *Le Mysteres du Chateau de De* 1929) which delivered little meaning and required viewer engagement to fill in gaps and to make the 'boring' interesting and worthwhile; to negotiate the separation between self and world. The plots of *Emak-Bakia* and *The Starfish* reflect the anomie of modern experience and offer us an opportunity to face our unsettling experience and respond by subjective meaning-making. *Emak-Bakia* contains (IMDB 2019):

A long series of unrelated images, revolving, often distorted: lights, flowers, nails. A lightboard appears from time to time carrying the news of the day. Then, an eye. A woman in a car drives along country roads. Farm animals. She descends from the car, again and again. Images: dancing legs, seashore, swimming fish, geometric shapes, cut glass. A man removes his starched collar. It rotates. A girl has garishly painted eyes. No, she's only fooling. Those were her eyelids.

While *The Starfish* relays the following unfolding (IMDB 2019):

Two people stand on a road, out of focus. Seen distorted through a glass, they retire upstairs to a bedroom where she undresses. He says, "Adieu". Images: the beautiful girl, a starfish in a jar, city scenes, newspapers, tugboats. More images: starfish, the girl. "How beautiful she is". Repeatedly.

He advances up the stair, knife in hand, starfish on the step. Three people stand on a road, out of focus. "How beautiful she was". "How beautiful she is". "Beautiful".

Unlike in pre-modern art which was presented as 'readymade' for consumption, appreciation, and entertainment, in these Dadaist films we are encouraged to acknowledge the inherent meaninglessness and unfinished nature of the plot (anomie) and are presented with the choice to resign ourselves to its meaninglessness or to complete the work through personal illumination.

There was an additional unprecedented consequence to this new movement, lamented internally within the art world and externally in mass society, which led to the fall of art's status as a dominant social institution. The price of famous modern art pieces rose precipitously and arbitrarily. Scribbles (*Painting Number 2* Franz Kline 1954), a blank canvas (*White Paintings* Rauschenberg 1951), a mass produced rabbit sculpture (Jeff Koons 1986), simple installations of lights turning on and off (*Work No. 227: The Lights Going On and Off* Creed 2000), or product taped to the wall (Maurizio Cattelan 2019), with the right famous autograph, could sell for hundreds of thousands and even millions of dollars. Hence, with the loss of standards, the price of art became a matter of status and name recognition and an extension of the artist's fame. Yet, each art object no longer held inherent value (of craftsmanship, technique, hours of production labor, traditionally-esteemed archetyping and iconography).

In another unprecedented turn, unlike with traditional fine art, value became determined by price (Kahn 2018). A 2018 documentary *The Price of Everything*'s refrains—"Some people know the price of everything, but the value of nothing", "Great things tell you they're great", and "The best art is the most expensive" (Kahn)—capture the new modus operandi of modern art. Contemporary art is similar to bitcoins for investors, sort of like a currency they invented themselves for their own purposes. One interviewee (Kahn 2018) captures the following popular sentiment of many in the film [paraphrased]:

> Prices are established by what the auctioneers, dealers, consigners think they're worth. There's more money out there than good art. I personally believe a lot of what dealers talk up as art to fill voids in availability is actually shit that won't stand the test of time. Very few people who are buying would meet the minimum standards of being considered a connoisseur!

The Price of Everything's standing theme is: There are no rules about what will be good and what will be bad, because art is art. With clear standards and the inherent value of art objects lost, and with much of production being 'aesthetically bankrupt', the status of fine art in Western society declined. It was no longer taken seriously and many have even gone so far to state that art is dead (Estrada-Salazer 2019).

As art has lost legitimacy, museums, the traditional sanctuaries and protectorates of fine art, have also suffered. Interest in art and museum patronage is down

(Kahn 2018). To stay afloat and to lure patrons, museums have been forced to transform into interactive entertainment businesses with elements of Las Vegas and Disney World, offering games and activities, further lowering arts legitimacy and its esteem with mass society (Kahn 2018).

These painting 'dialogues' leaves the viewer waiting and unsatisfied himself. Haladyn (2015) describes it well:

> what we are seeing is not so much that we are bored with the painting but rather that the painting is bored with us. (p. 52)
>
> [...]
>
> Aesthetic judgment thus affectively determines the experience and meaning of an encounter (p. 69)
>
> [...]
>
> [a]ctively takes on and reflects the perceived meaninglessness of lived existence in the modern world. As an acceptance of the futile quest to experience an objective sense of meaningfulness in a merely subjective world, boredom as an act of will affectively delineates the experiential parameters of the modernist aesthetic as a purposive failure of the subject to engage with or be engaged by the world. (p. 96).

With its emergence, artists from Man Ray to Andy Warhol, embraced the theme of boredom as an artistic concept. When you consider the purpose of fine art as an institution focused on maintaining the sensory interest of its audience, boredom's rendering becomes peculiar and perplexing. Why would the artist whose aim is to keep his viewer visually stimulated and interested, chose such a subject? Artists who chose the subject of boredom were simply echoing the soundtrack of their generation—a general sentiment of soullessness and emptiness. They created such art in an attempt to resolve the anomie of their society. It was a kind of crowdsourcing, searching for solutions for their cultural malaise. It was also a way of shaking up society, triggering self-awareness, and empowering their subject to become an active meaning-maker—an essential survival 'skill' in modernity. The consumption of modern art provided a training opportunity for 'getting' the essence of modernity (anomie) and encouraging the mastering of skills that were essential to greater societal adjustment.

As Haladyn (2015) suggests that to depict boredom, one had to experience and develop an eye for it. He writes of modernity:

> art becomes a vital source of ontological validation within a subjective world where previous objective structuring mechanisms such as religion and monarchies, which served as external causalities, fail to fulfill the requirements of an internalized causal view of subjectivity. This particular dynamic has continued to be a problem for modern existence... While celebrating its ability to create its own world and determine its own existence and sense of reality, humanity retains a base desire to externally substantiate and authenticate the real. (p. 42)

Haladyn is implying that art, by resembling and validating the experience of the observer, cushions the pain of anomie. It helps "negotiate the symptomatic separation of self and world" (Haladyn 2015, p. 43). In fact, the will to boredom becomes an important strategy of modern art, through the integration of boredom into its conceptual and temporal aspects.

Artists deliberately achieved boredom as an audience effect. Svendsen (2005) explains:

> In boredom, our gaze is somewhat similar to the objectivized look, in a purportedly pure perception where music is nothing but a series of sounds and a painting merely blotches of colour. In boredom events and objects are given to us as before, but with the important difference that they appear to have been stripped of meaning. (p. 109)

Contemporary art deliberately enacted simple method and composition to invoke meaninglessness and remind the audience of the temporal limits of aesthetic enjoyment. The new aesthetic emphasized that although art could help us experience sensory bliss and intoxication, its effect is temporary. Its stewards and movements efforted to make their production aesthetically forgettable and passable.

Aesthetic of indifference

Andy Warhol, as part of the post-war *Aesthetic of Indifference* movement, strategically used boredom in his films for engaging with the audience by serving as a catalyst for their self-awareness of their own expectations, limitations, and inner void. He famously remarked that he liked things boring (Warhol & Hacket 1980, p. 50): "I've been quoted a lot as saying, 'I like boring things'. Well I said it and I meant it. But that does not mean that I am not bored by them". Svendsen (2005) deconstructs Warhol's philosophy and emphasizes that the 800 dense pages of Warhol's diary repeat the word boring frequently and are notably boring to read. Just as his art production, they neither contain depth nor meaningfulness. He elaborates:

> What fascinates me most about Warhol is his uncompromising insistence on meaninglessness.... Warhol and his work are so flat they are completely transparent, just as pornography is. Baudrillard reckons that Warhol 'was the first person to bring us modern fetishism, transaesthetical fetishism—to a picture without quality, a presence without desire'. Warhol's art returns to a pre-Romantic paradigm of art, where expressiveness is not a relevant category. Warhol's work deals with the inner abstraction of things, with everything appearing as a flat echo of itself and Warhol empowering their spiritual emptiness. Apart from many of the paintings from the 1960s, especially the series of 'disaster paintings', there followed a monochrome canvas of the same size that further seems to underline the emptiness in the paintings.

Everything is dead in Warhol, although sometimes there is something beautiful as well—when he succeeds in portraying the shoddy with a cool purity. ... Warhol's art has to do with style and fashions, nothing else. He said: 'You can't be more superficial than me and live'. Warhol is devoid of any soul, and he removed the soul from everything he depicted, as is particularly obvious in the pictures of celebrities he did, when the person depicted has stiffened and become a flat icon, stripped of any depth. In the 15 minutes, it is the actual fame, not its content, that is of importance. Warhol's ideal picture of a human is an empty, impersonal figure that gains fame and makes a lot of money. He managed to fulfil this ambition himself, becoming something as paradoxical as an anonymous superstar. (pp. 101–102)

Warhol's self-defined philosophy of 'looking for nothingness' was advanced by his prints and films, which deliberately abstained from novelty, entertainment, and 'film effects' (ex. altering the camera's perspective and showing compelling images). Importantly, art became a commodity, just like his prints.

Rose (1965, p. 101 as quoted in McDonough 2017) describes Warhol's art:

Andy Warhol's Brillo boxes, silk screen paintings of the same image repeated countless times and films in which people or things hardly move are illustrations of the kind of life situations many ordinary people will face or face already.

Warhol's art was profoundly democratic in that it captured the ordinary and was seemingly accessible to anyone. Ironically, his obsession with nothingness penetrated his personality and reified him as a cult figure of non-personality. Svendsen (2005) describes:

but there is something paradoxical involved in doing away with one's own individuality, as Warhol attempted to do.... Warhol was himself well aware of this paradox. As he said in 1963: "I want everybody to think alike ... I think everybody should be a machine.... Everybody just goes on thinking the same thing, and every year it gets more and more alike. Those who talk about individuality are the ones who most object to deviation, and in a few years it may be the other way round." I believe Warhol was right in his prophecy here. Deviation has even become conformist. Everyone today has to be 'something special', without standing out in any way at all. Deviation is boring. When individualism is conformist, conformism also becomes individualistic.... Warhol demanded that his gravestone should not be inscribed, a demand that was not respected by his surviving relatives, but a blank stone would also have been a strongly individualistic move. (pp. 102–103)

By virtue of attempting to blend in and to hyper-conform, he overdid himself, and rose as an idol for individualism. Warhol's omission of himself invokes the pre-Enlightenment and pre-Romantic era prior to the emergence of individualism. Then, as creation was believed to be inspired by God, it was considered profane for artists to accept personal credit for and sign their work. Few respective pieces were marked with personal signature.

However, the major difference in pre-Enlightenment/pre-Romantic era and Warhol's work was symbology. Whereas the former invoked God and the Virgin for its audience of true believers, Warhol invoked common household items and redundant images of celebrities to the masses. Svendsen (2005) suggests that after the mid-1960s, Warhol's art grew "worse and worse" (p. 103) because his aesthetic symbols, with redundancy, lost their potency, and his art, stripped of romance and historicity, represented "sheer contemporaneity" (p. 105). In this respect, Warhol's art became a stronger expression of the *Aesthetic of Indifference*.

In line with the former observation, I would like the reader to consider Warhol from the concept of *conspicuous boredom*: maintaining the appearance of boredom in an attempt to enhance one's prestige and involving a philosophy of 'doing nothing'. Svendsen (2005) writes:

> He gained maximum benefit out of displaying his own boredom, wearing it like an expensive piece of jewelry. He is reminiscent of Paul Valéry's Monsieur Teste, who, devoid of content, is almost pure non-existence.... In boredom both the world and the personality are annihilated. (p. 106)

This level of uncompromising conformity allowed Warhol to play safe, as his art took few risks, while upholding his boredom as a status symbol. *He mastered the paradox of standing out for fitting in.* Khan (2011) writes on this particular skill of American elites. As opposed to French elites whose status is characterized by sophistication and highbrow activities, American elites pride themselves on their democratic attitude, dress, and tastes of enjoying both high-brow and low-brow culture. They 'perform' class and, paradoxically, enact huge efforts to style themselves in simple clothes, with the goal of mastering conformity and maintaining the status quo. Socially, successful elites acquire popularity for their skill of hyper-conformism. Warhol's personality and art carry such elements of hyper-conformism.

While most film makers aimed for entertainment, pleasure, distraction, transcending banality and entering another world, Warhol implemented the content, mechanics, and temporality of his films as a confrontation tool for awakening self-awareness and limitation. As he was satisfied with a positive reception from his elite circle, appealing to the masses and achieving the commercial success of his films seemed irrelevant. Furthermore, compared to the entertainment industry, there was a role-reversal in which he was uninterested in relating to his viewers. In a display of entitlement and power, he instead expected his viewers to connect with him. In a 1969 interview, Warhol (in McDonough 2017, p. 87) stated: "When people go to a show today they're never involved anymore. A movie like *Sleep* gets them, involved again. They get involved with themselves and they create their own entertainment". His subjects included following the banalities of a young lady[3] (waking, phone conversation, applying makeup, trying on outfits, etc.), a man eating a mushroom over 45 minutes,[4] silent close-ups of different couples kissing for 3.5 minutes over 50 a minute span,[5] a man sleeping for

5 hours and 20 minutes,[6] and 8 hours of silent black and white footage of the Empire State Building.[7]Svendsen (2005, p. 101) writes: "He talked about his own film *Kitchen* (1965) as 'illogical, without motivation or character and completely ridiculous. Very much like real life'". Warhol's films are characterized by long duration, monopolized by silent and motionless scenes with flickering that causes nondifferentiation of character and plot, and with limited symbolic representation. Yet, Warhol is a master of temporal cinematography in that he deliberately utilizes extended filming of stationary or banal subjects to limit stages of motion and rhythm. Even his temporality suggests anomie.

Importantly, his plots are often non-linear and flat with few happenings and cultural references. They almost 'feel' as if the character or subject is accidental and arbitrary to passing and recording time. The NY-based cultural critic Lin (2001) writes:

> Most of Warhol's films and writings are ostensibly vacant, auratic exercises in the ongoingness of waiting for something (which was usually nothing) to happen.... Most of Warhol's films are about people not changing because not changing was what most people do most of the time. Change is atypical. Not changing is also known as boredom.

To complement the monotony of his plot, he often positions the camera stationary and out of focus, leaving forms shapeless and disembodied, depicting a visually monotonous experience (Haladyn 2015).

Another Warhol film critic states: "Most of your films have little or no editing. You keep the camera in one spot and keep shooting until the reels run out. Your characters enter and leave the frame. But there's no cutting, just reels spliced together" (Warhol and Gelmis 1969, p. 87 in McDonough 2017). Unlike mainstream film, which utilizes elements of temporal cinematography (i.e. regular and unpredictable novelty, change of subject and objects, interesting movement, unexpected composition) to create meaningful rhythm and enliven the narrative, Warhol deliberately curates the content and stylistic elements of shooting to assure us that his films 'keep it simple' and confront the viewer with the 'everyday' experiences of their own eyes—without distraction.

Such cinematography encourages his viewer to understand the emotional cost and 'emptiness' of engaging in daily banalities. Haladyn (2015) writes:

> In Warhol films perception is defined through a repetition of an ordered indifference, which actively prevents viewers from being distracted by the illusionism of the cinema. Instead, we engage in a project of endurance that tests the limits of our willingness to watch. (p. 156)

Warhol's films are curated to induce unsettling boredom. Lin (2001) comments on the temporality of his films:

> The films (like his novel A) are experiments in slowing down viewing (or reading) time or creating a lag between clock time and the rate at which we

register perceptual changes. One of the things that slow-motion does is make change harder to see. Oddly, boredom, which most people associate with things not changing, creates for Warhol a heightened state of anticipation, a place where beauty might erupt.... A typical Warhol film was shot at sound speed or 24 frames per second, but played back at silent speed, or 16 frames per second, thus literally slowing down the rate at which an image changes and prolonging the rate at which things stay the same. The slower speed enabled Warhol to capture what he called .nothing.: "we ran it at a slower speed to make up for the film I didn't shoot". The slowed-down film heightens the fact that something that we can't quite perceive or register is going on in the background, something unnoticed like wallpaper or something accidentally recorded, like off-screen voices.

Hence, Warhol artificially constructed temporality to create a 'boring' yet provocative effect, with both the substance and duration of his films advancing his agenda.

Common expectations of artistic modification and decorum, beauty, fantasy, illusion, entertainment, sensation, pleasure, and linear plot with meaningful narratives and references are denied: "Viewers expecting the illusion typical of Hollywood cinema were bored, just as Warhol intended" (Gardiner and Haladyn 2017, p. 68). In order for his films to be sensical, engaging, and interesting, the viewer personalize Warhol's films with his own story and meaning.

Many contemporary films have continued to integrate elements of the *aesthetic of indifference*. For example, the 1996 Cannes award winning film *Crash* (Cronenberg), which portrays auto collision, injury, death, and its eroticization, continues in the spirit of Man Ray and Warhol. It frames pleasure as an extension of danger and risk of death. *Crash* uses few special effects such as explosions and temporal modification (slow motion) that would entertain and encourage commercial success. Importantly, its characters are painfully bored with life and deliberately orchestrate auto crashes and its sequelae of risk, injury, and death to feel raw intensity, sexual arousal, and relief from the existential boredom of their regular life. Its sexual scenes consist of emotionless mechanical penetration instead of true sensual connection and soulful love making. Carnal activity is saturated with emptiness and boredom: there is no relational bonding, no eye contact, no titillating foreplay. Svendson (2005) coins the term *taedium sexualitatis* to describe their sexual boredom. He quotes an archetypal narrative from the film (p. 86): "I thought of my last forced orgasms with Catherine, the sluggish semen urged into her vagina by my bored pelvis". Its characters feel a breakdown of capacity in the own body—a type of bodily anomie or dérèglement, from Mestrovic's (1993) perspective, and require a bionic extension (automobile/auto cash) to feel sexual arousal and climax.

I coin the term *anomic sexual dysphoria* (ASD) to capture the experience of feeling confused, uncomfortable, and ashamed with one's sexual capacity and/or expression of sexual pleasure. This condition is characterized by either feeling numbness or immense distress around sexual performance/expression, fear around the incapacity to achieve arousal and climax, and tendency to compensate with the use of bionic extensions such as 'sex toys', games, or virtual reality that are violent and cause pain or with psychoactive substances. The motivation driving the latter is not to enhance enjoyment per se, but to conceal or compensate for an acutely distressing fear of incapacity with an overwhelmingly intense/painful experience. Hence, ASD is teleologically characterized by attempted transgressions from emotional numbness or acute distress vis-à-vis real or virtually simulated violent acts which deliberately cause pain or with psychoactive substances. This is a subset of anomie which permeates bodily experience (*bodily anomie*) and leads to sexual deviance whereby one needs outside overwhelming force to engage in sex. The characters of *Crash* suffer from this type of sexual dysfunction.

The musical composer John Cage was another household name associated with the *Aesthetic of Indifference*. He was known for silent music concerts during which neither deliberate nor arranged sound was produced, and background noise remained the only sound. He reified non-deliberate and unarranged sound, such as in his famous empty performance titled *4'33"* (1952), during which musicians are physically present for the performance without producing sound, while the audience attunes itself to natural background noise. The performance lasts for four minutes and thirty-three seconds. Cage (1961) states:

> In Zen they say: If something is boring after two minutes, try it for four. If still boring, try it for eight, sixteen, thirty-two, and so on. Eventually one discovers that it is not boring at all but very interesting. (p. 93)

His purpose was to confront his audience with their own capacity to face the 'seeming' silence and to learn to listen. Sontag ([1967] 2002) explains:

> As Cage insisted, "There is no such thing as silence. Something is always happening which makes a sound." (Cage has described how, even in a soundless chamber, he still heard two things (his heartbeat and the coursing of blood in his head.).... A genuine emptiness, a pure silence are not feasible either conceptually or in fact. If only because the artwork exists in a world furnished with many other things, the artist who creates silence or emptiness must produce something dialectical: a full void, an enriching emptiness, a resonating or eloquent silence. (pp. 10–11)

He believed that "No one can have an idea once he starts really listening" (Sontag [1967] 2002, p. 10). Cage's compositions denied heretofore assumptions about music as being deliberately composed of arranged melodious rhythmic sound, being stimulating, evoking particular emotions, entertaining, and *adding* sound.

Some of his performances played with the musicians' and audiences' thresholds for boredom versus intensity. In one performance, Cage orchestrated two musicians to simultaneously play their own pieces in the dark so that the audience would be unable to guess its beginning and ending, which induced vacillating feelings of boredom and intensity (Higgins 1968 as referenced in McDonough 2017). Hence, Cage dismissed classic assumptions about compositional development and the temporal distribution of musical events, as well as the audience's expectations regarding the beginning and completion of performance.

In line with the *Aesthetic of Indifference*, Cage and other artists of the movement, deliberately chose to democratize notes, not privileging any one note or any one refrain over another. Sontag ([1967] 2002, p. 25) describes its creed: "The function of art isn't to sanction any specific experience, except for the state of being open to the multiplicity of experience—which ends in practice by a decided stress on things usually considered trivial or unimportant". Kania (2017, p. 357) emphasizes: "improvisation is one kind of music-making that collapses the distinction between the specific temporal properties of the musical event one experiences directly and the determinable temporal properties of a work for performance". If music is the art of sound and time (Levinson 1990), the movement's respective musicians were successful in manipulating both elements of composition.

In fact, they were in conversation with modernity and its soundtrack of over-stimulation. It aimed to serve as a counter balance to the hyperactive and enervating tempo of accelerated time. While most people were being bombarded with over-stimulation and driven to do *more, faster*, musicians of this trend used minimalistic sound or 'silence' to invoke a sense of stilling and slowing time. Sontag ([1967] 2002, p. 21) explains: "In an overpopulated world being connected by global electronic communication and jet travel at a pace too rapid and violent for an organically sound person to assimilate without shock". The counterbalancing agenda of the *Aesthetic of Indifference*, although compelling, failed to relay its message clearly.

Its performances were lost to many viewers and were seen as insulting and as passive-aggressive (McDonough 2017). Some did not take well to purchasing tickets and devoting their evening to 'listening' to experimental silence. As they could have remained home and accomplished the same for free, spectators felt confused and deceived. Hence, the reception of the movement was mixed and largely lost to audiences (McDonough 2017). It could also be said that although this movement aimed at democratizing 'sound' and making it accessible to all, by deliberately omitting tradition, history, familiar references, and by reproducing certain elite musical style trends, it was inherently bourgeois. What echelon of people can afford to purchase tickets and devote time for a prolonged multi-hour concert (some of which lasted for about 20 hours)? Although this movement was fascinating and had its converts, its reach was farther than its grasp.

The *Aesthetic of Indifference* also influenced visual art. Robert Rauschenberg painted in its spirit and was well known for producing blank white paintings that are uniform in size (1951). John Cage ([1953] Roberts 2013) responded to Rauschenberg's production with a haiku:

To whom

No subject

No image

No taste

No object

No beauty

No message

No talent

No technique (no why)

No idea

No intention

No art

No feeling

No black

No white

(No and) ...

John Cage gave language to this artistic movement, which made a statement of non-statement, and further confronted its viewership with nothingness. Narusyte (2010) writes:

> 'the aesthetic of silence' in which artists and writers avoided saying something meaningful and destroyed the foundations of art, yet also brought about a new kind of art that questioned ideas about the human mind and offered a new conception and language ... the refusal to speak was not just a gesture of indifference or silence, but a 'performance of silence' ... or 'indecisiveness' over what to say when the subject was constantly in the process of being 'read' by the other. In such a situation an author would pass the task of creating meaning over to the context or to the spectator ... this new art does not speak in the usual way. (pp. 14–15)

Painters of the *Aesthetic of Indifference*, like Rauschenberg, opted out of the normal strategies of visual art—the deliberate arrangement of color possibly for decorative purposes, expression of particular emotions and setting a mood, complexity of form and color, incorporating meaningful references, and general sensory stimulation—resulting in a major paradigm shift. Former assumptions were negated, and art as we knew it died. This movement accomplished simplicity and singularity by minimizing the use of color, creating symmetrical and systematic compositions (Gardiner and Haladyn 2017) with repetition. "Because Minimal artworks 'discourage expectations of formal complexity', they were often accused of being boring" (Gardiner and Haladyn 2017, p. 69). Its reception included confusion, restlessness, as well as personal empowerment. Rose

(1965, p. 100 as quoted in McDonough 2017) describes its withdrawal of content:

> That these young artists attempt to suppress or withdraw content from their works is undeniable. That they wish to make art that is as bland, neutral and as redundant as possible also seems clear. Then content, then, if we are to take the work at face value, should be nothing more than the total of the series of assertions that it is this or that shape and takes up so much space and is painted such a colour and made of such a material. Statements from the artists involved are frequently couched in these equally factual, matter-of-fact descriptive terms; the work is described but not interpreted and statements with regard to content or meaning or intention are prominent only by their omission.

Just as with its musical branch, visual artists of this movement aimed to democratize fine art by creating in the style of a blank slate, open to 'anything'.

By rejecting tradition and heretofore systems of knowledge and hierarchies of quality, they aimed to make art accessible to all. However, from the outset, their endeavor was set to fail. While the average person may relate to depictions of the Virgin Mary because of their circulation in popular culture media and because of her family and community heritage, she may not relate to or see a purpose in 'searching for meaning' in a blank white slate, let alone in paying for admission for a viewing. The average person cannot, financially or time-wise, afford such boredom, and if she finds herself there, may feel uncomfortable in said 'pretentious setting' where most are pretending to see depth and value in 'nothing'. Hence, the minimalism branch of the *Aesthetic of Indifference* was more bourgeois and less accessible than the traditional art that it rejected.

The movement continued to influence choreography. Merce Cunningham, a 'non-representational' choreographer, rose to fame for deliberate omission of representation of events, ideas, and emotional experience, for his deliberate failure to coordinate dance with music (dancing 'with' music but not 'to' music), indeterminacy: using spontaneous chance sequencing of dance moves (moves are decided by chance), and for omission of sequence and plot: a beginning, middle, climax, and ending in his dance repertoires. As an example, the dance *Canfield* (1969) used indeterminacy by assigning a movement to a playing card and randomly choosing one (Au 1988). Bresnahan (2017) describes the temporal element of contemporary dance:

> Some dancers, particularly in contemporary dance, may train without music (using breath, foot, or body impacts for the beat, for example) or to less beat-driven music, but even here there is usually some sort of time parameter that emerges. In addition, timing of movements and rests may be set by the choreographer for performance, or left open or more variable (as in improvisational dance). Dancers may also experience the temporal parameters of moving in synchronization with or in conjunction with other dancers.

In general, fast tempos require what dancers call 'attack' and energy in the movements. For a movement to be quicker in tempo, a dancer might need either a smaller movement or a greater amount of force behind the movement.... Once a dancer has trained to do certain movements in a certain tempo his body and brain become accustomed to that tempo and the movements become easier to perform. Performing repeated longer-duration movements that allow for greater extension, for example, make it easier and easier for the dancer to perform those movements ... the dancer is extremely and excruciatingly aware of passing from one step or movement to the next in both time and in space.... It is this physicality, among other things, that marks the temporal moments as significant for the dancer, and they come forward in her consciousness as moments and she feels them as part of a whole dance. In addition, thinking-while-dancing takes place in an ever-changing present of which she is aware even while it is constantly changing. ... This is particularly true during dance improvisations or in improvisational moments of a set dance. (pp. 340–343)

Although contemporary dancers may synchronize their movements to music and allow music to temporally organize their repertoire, such congruence is not necessary in 'non-representational' choreography, deeming it experientially and temporally anomic.

The composer Robert Dunn describes a 'non-representational' piece he choreographed at the Merce Cunningham's New York dance studio (Rose 1965, p. 101 as quoted by McDonough 2017):

in a solo called *The Bells* I repeated the same seven movements for eight minutes. It was not exact repetition, as the sequence of the movements kept changing. They also underwent changes through being repeated in different parts of the space and faced in different directions—in a sense allowing the spectator to 'walk around it'.

In *The Bells* we see very clearly, that unlike in traditional art and dance which is 'readymade' with a clear engaging plot, a beginning, middle, climax, and end, and during which the audience is positioned in a stationary spot with the 'best view' for watching and enjoyment, in modern dance, such assumptions are omitted, and even the audience can stand and watch from wherever they please—creating the possibility for anomie and boredom. Dance, in the spirit of the *Aesthetic of Indifference*, usually enacts many common movements, such as walking, in slow motion, as opposed to the highly refined movement of classical ballet. Critically, unlike in traditional ballet which includes a hierarchy of dancers with a 'prima ballerina' reified as 'the best' and irreplaceable for her talent, modern dance, being experimental without clear standards of quality, is democratic, and dancers tend to be fairly interchangeable with one another. Sontag ([1967] 2002, p. 13) writes: "The alternative view denies the traditional hierarchies of interest and meaning, in which some things have more 'significance' than others... in principle, one should desire to pay attention to everything". Hence, even modern art's standards (or lack thereof) tend to anomic, as anything goes and can be judged, as worthy or not, subjectively at whim.

Overall, *The Aesthetic of Indifference* magnetized mixed reviews and was hugely misunderstood. As its guiding principles were problematic, it was wrought with difficulty from the onset. It was led by beliefs that:

1 *The public's crisis of meaning could be resolved through observing and engaging with the Aesthetic of Indifference.* However, as this genre failed to direct the viewer through a clear resolution process, invoking further feelings of anomie, and as anomie cannot resolve itself, most viewers were left confused, impatient, disappointed, and even with a sense of spiritual or "suicidal vertigo" (Sontag [1967] 2002). In fact, the *aesthetic of indifference* left many with amplified and unresolved anomie, repelling them from art and from the art world. And let us consider that many artists of this movement died of overdoses and suicide. Hence, many leaders of this movement were severely troubled and unable to use their own medicine to heal themselves, suggesting that it was hugely ineffective in resolving anomie.

2 *The public prefers art that rejects tradition and cultural symbolism versus art that incorporates it.* However, most prefer art with some level of familiarity and recognizable cultural reference. Audiences generally seek art that is profoundly inspiring whose beauty and power invoke deep feeling. Art that rejects tradition would only resonate with those who have consciously rejected tradition.

3 *Art is a good medium to relay meaning and purpose.* However, language is the most precise symbolic system we have for relaying precise meaning. And even language is often imprecise and leads to miscommunication. Compared to language, art is at a disadvantage as its symbols have not been reified and universally accepted. As a consequence, the viewership of this movement was often found confused and disappointed (McDonough 2017), and never came to consider its potential and purpose for resolving anomie.

The Russian case

> Every work of art is the child of its age, and in many cases, the mother of our emotions. It follows that each period of culture produces an art of its own which can never be repeated.
>
> Kandinsky 1977

From the West, an interest in producing deliberately boring art spread to the Soviet Union (Narusyte 2010) as part of the Non-Official Art,[8] Soviet Non-Conformist Art Movement, and the genre of Soviet Conceptual Art. And just as their Western counterparts, Soviet artists reflected their own grey monotony by regularly invoking the theme of boredom in aesthetic representation. Their work was set against the propagandistic backdrop of the pageantry of red marches and heroic speeches. As Kandinsky's quote above suggests (1977), Soviet artists wanted to echo the actual reality which was eerily and painfully empty, full of large grey cement and empty landscape. Riesman ([1950] 2001): writes:

> Modern totalitarianism is also more inefficient and corrupt than it is often given credit for being, but its aims are unlimited and for this reason it must wage total war on autonomy.... For the autonomous person's acceptance of social and political authority is always conditional: he can cooperate with others in action while maintaining the right of private judgment. There can be no recognition whatever of such a right under totalitarianism—one reason why in the Soviet Union artistic works and scientific theories are so relentlessly scrutinized for 'deviationism', lest they conceal the seeds even of unconscious privacy and independence of perception. (p. 250)

Soviet artists were radically in touch with their independent perception. They aimed for inner-directed expression and radical autonomy. Most were met with strong resistance from the State.

Ilya Kabakov was an exception. His interactions with the government were deliberately conformist (PBS 2005). He joined the Union of Soviet Artists and avoided engaging with political ideology; this move granted him a state salary and protected him from persecution, allowing him to continue to make art. Through conceptual and installation techniques, Ilya deliberately engaged with the subject of boredom and hopeless boredom. In his 1972–1975 work titled *Albums* Kabakov created an illustration of a series of fictional characters who are overcome by boredom. The series begins with an illustration of a man who thinks about writing his autobiography until he realizes that very little noteworthy happened. It continues by depicting characters of people whose lives are insignificant and empty, serving as a stark contrast to Soviet propaganda. There are no interesting or meaningfully-engaged figures in his work, possibly suggesting his commentary on boredom being the only option in the Soviet Union (Narusyte 2010). In his 1992 installation *The Life of Flies* Kabakov depicts four windowless dull-lit grey-walled halls in a provincial museum in which the atmosphere is so hopelessly boring that even flies die from it. Collaterally, the exhibits of the museum are meant to intensity boredom; they consist of anonymous objects like rocks and horns. The piece deliberately invokes boredom by creating a non-stimulating atmosphere (Kabakov 1992).

The paintings of dissident Oscar Rabin, known as the 'Solzhenitsyn of Painting', and one of the original leaders of the Soviet Non-Conformist Art Movement, serve as another notable example (Genzlinger 2018). He mastered echoing the depressingly industrial dreary mood of the 1960s and 70s. Eventually, he was confronted and beaten by police, imprisoned, and exiled abroad.

While Boris Mikhailov is best known for photographing images of the homeless, their children, and those living on the fringes of society. He captures his subjects in vulnerable poses and nude, aiming to relay their destitution and desperation, at the throws of anomic dissolving Soviet society. Focusing on the everyday and on boring elements of Soviet and Russian life, his mostly black and white photography serves to shatter the narrative of the government propaganda machine and serves to capture the disenchanted state of mind of millions of Soviet citizens (Effimova 1994).

In terms of photography, in Lithuania, art photographers[9] from 1980 to 1990 adopted boredom as an aesthetic category with the dual intent of subtly rejecting the conventions and fictions of Soviet ideology and of high culture (Narusyte 2010). It was a silent revolution with a political purpose. Ontologically, it invited conceptual interpretation. Agne Narusyte, an art critic and curator, suggests the term 'social landscape', which indirectly expresses the author's perspective by integrating elements of conceptualism and documentary photography of the "imperfect 'here and now'" (p. 27) to capture this new wave of deadpan images of household items, furniture, chance/accidental moments, and blurred/bizarre landscapes. Their attitude was generally impartial, passionless, anonymous, ironic, interpretive, and defensive of portraying imperfect reality, with no humanitarian ethos of aiding those living at the margins.

Viewers were invited to meditate on overlooked aspects of their everyday experience: "a process which softens the edges of art; diluting daily experience with eternity" (p. 27) and leads to "elevated states of mind" (p. 30). The 'social landscape' movement aimed to sever ties with traditional social photography which was driven by a commitment to humanitarianism. It began in Vilnius and spread throughout Lithuania. Narusyte (2010) describes its dissent:

> The monotonous photographs of dull cityscapes and other mundane images suggested that these young photographers were openly antagonistic towards the creation of optimistic images of a progressive society and even, possibly, criticizing the existing situation. However, it was also obvious that the idealism and the undeclared purpose of the older generation to resist occupation and preserve national values by documenting Lithuanian rural traditions and people, did not interest these young photographers either. From the traditional point of view, the new photography lacked meaning, ideas and a sense of purpose, hence it was essentially empty. The spectator's confusion in the face of this lack was expressed by the first critics of this photography. They declared that the young photographers were 'disassociating themselves from human beings and socially important phenomena'; that they were 'not very interested in the dynamic action of life, the journey of human life, social and psychological things' or that the 'unease caused by the insufficient social contents of these photographers is quite founded'. (pp. 18–21)

This new movement focused on relaying the authentic 'essence' of context and objects. Narusyte (2010, p. 21) explains: "They resented banality of thinking, cheap aesthetic staging and falsity covered with a decorative mask of optimism". These young photographers considered stereotypical and idealized symbols of spiritual and physical beauty and the promotion of national identity inherently wrong.

They chose to forgo idealized, clear, and banal captures of the countryside and the peasant and relay the degradation of the city—the material environment of their youth.

While at first glance this new genre offered "experiences that seemed to have no value were offered instead" (Narusyte 2010, p. 21), "their emergence in photography was neither accidental nor without purpose. This emergence was related to changes in attitudes and the radically different perception of identity that was held by the photographers" (p. 23). Their work upheld ambivalence, blurred and disintegrating boundaries, scratched and overdeveloped images exhibited in a chaotic manner, as an ideal. Old criteria, of precise representation and elegant composition was inadequate at distilling meaning from this new genre. At first impression, their viewership may see 'creative failures', 'poor quality', 'boring' images, and 'trash' not worthy of their attention. Full understanding of this new genre was highly case-by-case and depended on engaging personally with each artist.

Importantly, the 'social landscape' movement's refusal to record specific social and biographical events and articulate a straightforward mission, maintained the self-preservation of its members within the totalitarian Soviet context. Those seemingly lacking a clear history with a clear message are harder to target, oppress, and destroy. Their silent revolution was subtle and softly implied through the mystery and poetry of their monotonous images. As similar movements of indifference to convention, the 'social landscapes' wave severed ties with its traditional past.

A critical difference between the ethos of traditional art and the modern creed of 'making art boring' was that the former extended from collectivism in which meanings were experienced through the unison of predictable and shared understanding while the latter extended from radical individualism which reified the subjective and ontologically sought interpretation on a person-to-person and moment-to-moment basis. While a marked difference between aesthetic depictions of boredom in Anglo and Russian society was that the former confronted its audience with 'nothing', while many artists of the latter portrayed empty human lives and relayed specific points, risking their own life. American artists quietly echoed the anomie of their environment and opted out of direct social commentary and political confrontation, obfuscating their true intentions of social critique coupled with revolutionary self-awareness and social change. They were viewed as avant-garde, controversial, mysterious, confusing, and as pretentious non-art. Meanwhile, Soviet conceptual art, with the exception of Lithuanian photography, was inherently confrontational and placed the artist and his audience in danger. Expressing social and politically unflattering commentary and portraying society as boring was not tolerated by the government establishment. The Soviet artist operated in a rigidly defined space of the allowances and limits of 'art'. Departing from its rules meant attack, imprisonment, and exile. And yet, the Soviet artist was so powerfully motivated by his anomic predicament of societal disintegration that he could not help risk his life screaming his reflections.

The future of art

Fine art in the spirit of the renaissance is more than just its aesthetic production, it maintained the original values of Western civilization for centuries. Although the renaissance-derived institution of art is gone, isolated individuals who continue to practice art, as well as art historians, remain vestiges of a recently forgotten world. These individuals need to recognize their role in maintaining and reviving fine art both for its rich potential for enjoyment and for its systematic process of creation and knowledge of us as a civilization. Unlike modern art, in the spirit of the *Aesthetic of Indifference*, which failed to offer a cohesive system for development and continuation, as well as intrinsic sensory enjoyment, meaning, a sense of belonging, and historical knowledge, art in the spirit of the renaissance, which lasted for approximately 600 years, gifted its community and progeny with morals, beauty in form, and clarified our identity and confidence as a Western Civilization. Contemporaneously, general art education, with an inclusion of Renaissance art and art history, should be offered from pre-school. A strong knowledge of art and art history would allow for a clarification of our historical identity, societal cohesion, and a revival in confidence.

Art education in the US is limited. Even schools which fund art mostly focus on arts-and-crafts, aesthetics, and specific elements and mechanical techniques such as color theory, texture, shape, pointillism and printmaking, at the exclusion of 'fine art' and its historical context. Little significance is attributed to the individual artist, his *raison d'etre*, and the relationship between him and his zeitgeist. Such a presentation of 'art' is a consequence of the breakdown of its institution. As a consequence of the breakdown of this institution, art teachers are left to their own devices, and many focus on their personal subjective interests and teach techniques such as imitation and encourage students to open-endedly and without context to 'do whatever you want'. For the revival of fine art in the spirit of the renaissance, there needs to be a group of willing passionate artists and art historians who develop an educational program solidifying its creed, standards, and practices, and making it relevant for the current generation. This community would need to expand its influence and implement its curriculum within the school system and revive enthusiasm for the joy and value of fine art throughout society.

Notes

1 Quote from Cheng (2007).
2 This tenet was an attempt to rebel against blind consumerism and engage in class warfare. Artists aim to transcend the pressure to create art that is easily appealing and profitable. The, potentially unintended, consequence of this tenet is the alienation of the institution of art and its aesthetic products from the masses, and the decline of art's status in society.
3 *Poor Little Rich Girl* (1965).
4 *Eat* (1963).
5 *Kiss* (1963).
6 *Sleep* (1963).

7 *Empire* (1964).
8 In the Soviet Union, there was a distinction between 'official art' which was created within and for government initiatives, such as for the production of cartoons or children's books, and 'non-official art' which was produced privately, often in secret, as releasing such art could expose the artist to persecution. The only art officially sanctioned by the government was known as Soviet Union Socialist Realism. After the fall of the USSR, 'unofficial art' from the Soviet era was allowed global display.
9 Art photography refers to photography in which the art aesthetic is critical; it excludes photography for documentation and information purposes.

4 The boredom of politics

Explaining attraction to charismatic and violent rule

Boredom is always the external surface of unconscious events.

Walter Benjamin

War is long periods of boredom punctuated by moments of sheer terror.

Unknown

I think the biggest relationship was whether people had really routine jobs in an area and that correlated highly with Trump support versus having non-routine jobs. There's actually quite a bit of historical precedent for boredom being a huge factor in the vote choice and in building extremism. Actually, we've had a lot of work on jigsaw on extremism that shows high correlation to simple boredom.... Data suggests that boredom led to the rise of fascism and to the communist revolution.

Sergey Brin, Leaked Internal Google Video[1]

Boredom is often imagined as a passive waiting. However, as discussed in former chapters, it is both an emotion which can evolve into a heavy pathological state as well as an emotion of potentiality, with countless possibilities of resolution. Generally, when we consider politics and its sequalae, boredom is a rare association. Yet, research demonstrates that boredom has served as the political stage's atmosphere in key political processes: the expansion of empire, the election of charismatic leaders, the decision to enter war, attraction, recruitment, and the rejection of extremism such as Nazism, and participation in jihadi extremist groups, and of effective political strategy. Importantly, the political realm provides a fascinating case of the juxtaposition of normally polarizing emotions: boredom and terror.

Boredom within 19th century British colonialism

I use the case of boredom during 19th century British colonialism to establish boredom within the realm of politics and political activism. Many are all familiar with the romanticized propaganda of British colonialism as a thrilling adventure of exposure to the exotica of tribal people and to its abhorrent and anachronistic creed of civilizing the barbarian, yet primary source accounts of public servants sent to expand the empire and stationed abroad paint an image of its trappings: painful disenchantment and boredom (Aerbach 2018).

British public servants stationed overseas often found themselves with unfulfilling work and little else to do. According to personal diaries, letters, and memoirs, they were indifferent to their host culture. They entered an anomic situation which led to chronic feelings of boredom. George Orwell ([1934] 2018) in *Burmese Days* coins this experience of anomie and boredom as "Pox Britannica": the archetypal disease of the British sent abroad. In fact, according to Orwell's depiction, male public servants often had nothing left to do but drink themselves to death. Orwell (p. 39) commented: "of course drink is what keeps the machine going". Hence, a political movement: British colonialism sent representatives abroad to advance its mission.

Yet, stewards rarely felt connected to the foreign culture and its people, they were both unable to apply their British way of doing things in the host society and to find a new way of relating to their novel circumstances. Aerbach (2018) explains:

> Also important was the growth of British communities overseas, which grew progressively more isolated from indigenous people and customs. Increasingly, British men and women sought to re-create the very conditions they had left behind in a futile search for the familiarity of home, neither fully embracing nor entirely rejecting the newness and differences they encountered overseas.... In this respect boredom sheds light on a profound question that surfaced with great urgency in the nineteenth-century British Empire: How should one spend one's time? If boredom serves as a defense against the annoyance of waiting, this was something British men and women did a lot of in the nineteenth century: waiting for a ship to arrive, waiting for a military posting, waiting for a meeting to take place. As David Carnegie, a young colonial official who died in Northern Nigeria in 1900 when he and a group of armed men were ambushed while trying to catch a thief, complained to his mother soon after he arrived, "Job was a patient man, but I feel sure he was never on the Niger. The motto for this country ought to be 'Nothing matters, nobody cares, time's no object' ".[2] His annoyance over the uncertainty of the mail service and his frustration at "stewing away doing all sorts of jobs that seem of little importance" rather than fighting for his country in the Boer War is palpable. Only his confessions of boredom seem to keep his anger or sense of uselessness in check. (p. 5)

Many stationed abroad were left feeling unstimulated, ineffective, and paralyzed, and coped through alcohol.

Nineteenth century colonialism also suffered from its advertising campaign which left countless with unfulfilled expectations and drove a sense of meaninglessness. Aerbach (2018) elaborates:

> Boredom can also be seen as a crisis of unfulfilled or unacknowledged desire. In this way, boredom is intimately linked to expectations, which in the

imperial context were heightened by propagandistic pamphlets, popular paintings and engravings, and self-serving memoirs. Hunters rarely found big game; diggers rarely struck gold. As it turns out, British men and women in the nineteenth century found it remarkably difficult to enjoy their imperial present.... "There is nothing to look back upon", Augusta King confessed in the diary she kept during her five years in India from 1877 to 1882, "and nothing to look forward to", only "absolute monotony".[3] (pp. 5–6)

He emphasizes that several elements of colonialism were especially boring: monotonous ocean travel by steamship, viewing, governing, defending, and settling the British Empire. In the 19th century, the steamship was invented and safety and navigation routes improved. This led to ocean travel becoming normalized with clear routes, few stops, and minimal scenery of land and animals. Travel became less dangerous and less interesting. Additionally, voyage times generally took three to six months during which passengers were isolated from their close ones back home and only had each other (with whom they were generally strangers) for socializing. This led to passengers of all ranks to regularly complain of monotony and boredom (Aerbach 2018). In this case, we clearly see how unorganized time with strangers (community anomie) and long-distance time (temporality) led to boredom.

Aerbach (2018) emphasizes that as Britain transitioned from relying on indigenous rulers to their own stationed administrators and civil servants, governing became increasingly bureaucratic with huge amounts of paperwork and deskwork, affecting their sense of mission and purpose. Additionally, most were stationed in the countryside where the landscape and lifestyle were remembered as torturous, savage, uninspiring, uninviting, drab, monotonous, and boring (Aerbach 2018). There were particularly gendered consequences for men and women. In terms of masculinity and defense, Aerbach (2018) explains:

Although the story of the British Empire has often been told in terms of its military campaigns … and although military heroism was part of the lore of the British Empire, by the mid-nineteenth century soldiers were spending much of their time sitting in tents in the heat with little to do but drink. Many soldiers, in fact, went years, and in some cases decades, without participating in so much as a skirmish. As the empire grew in size, there were more and more British soldiers stationed overseas, and with the army's enormous advantage in firepower, especially following the invention of the repeating rifle, battles were shorter and more one-sided. These changes in warfare, and the huge increase in references to boredom that resulted from them, also align closely with new definitions of masculinity, suggesting that the boredom soldiers expressed was at least partly related to their inability to demonstrate their bravery and physical prowess in the absence of hand-to-hand combat. In the end, many found themselves deeply disillusioned with imperial service. The well-known saying that war consists of "Months of boredom punctuated by moments of terror", a phrase first used by a British officer stationed on the Western Front during the First World War, had its figurative origins in the nineteenth-century British Empire. (p. 8)

The mentioned combination of widespread boredom and terror also characterizes war (Maeland & Brunstad 2009), the hostage situation of 9/11 (Amis 2009), and Stalinism (Bellow ([1975] 2008). British soldiers stationed abroad expected to conquer, fight, demonstrate bravery, and achieve heroism.

However, with the invention of firearms and repeating rifles, which the indigenous did not possess, hand-to-hand combat virtually ceased and most battles ended before beginning. Soldiers had few, if any, opportunities to enact battle and masculinity, and most spent their careers attempting to drink away their boredom. British women living in the colonies faced their own gendered boredom. Aerbach (2018) explains:

> Life was particularly difficult for women, whether entertaining friends in the Indian hill stations or whiling away the hours in the Australian outback. The former suffered from vapid social rituals and prohibitions on contact with indigenous people; the latter from extreme isolation and loneliness. With few exceptions, women, regardless of their social class, had lots of leisure time; the difficulty was filling it. They read; they painted; and they gossiped with other women, assuming there were any around. But all the parties in the world could not make up for the boredom, and in remote locations especially, the same people met day after day to eat the same meals and exchange the same tired conversation.[4] From Governors' wives to governesses, from gold diggers to bushwhackers, boredom was omnipresent. (p. 9)

Difficulty filling time is an inherently anomic problem. Women and men, living in the colonies experienced inadequate structural direction without clearly defined social roles.

Boredom within the electorate and the election of charismatic leaders

In *Economy and Society*, Weber famously defines the concept of charisma and its relationship to charismatic leadership. He writes ([1922] 1987):

> The term 'charisma' will be applied to a certain quality of an individual personality by virtue of which he is considered extraordinary and treated as endowed with supernatural, superhuman, or at least specifically exceptional powers or qualities. These are such as are not accessible to the ordinary person, but are regarded as of divine origin or as exemplary, and on the basis of them the individual concerned is treated as a "leader". In primitive circumstances this peculiar kind of quality is thought of as resting on magical powers, whether of prophets, persons with a reputation for therapeutic or legal wisdom, leaders in the hunt, or heroes in war. How the quality in

question would be ultimately judged from any ethical, aesthetic, or other such point of view is naturally entirely indifferent for the purposes of definition. What is alone important is how the individual is actually regarded by those subject to charismatic authority, by his "followers" or "disciples"....
Value-free sociological analysis will treat all these on the same level as it does the charisma of men who are the "greatest" heroes, prophets, and saviors according to conventional judgements. (pp. 241–242)

Weber's charisma is an in-born personality trait which expresses itself in unreflective contagious enthusiasm and natural authority. It spreads "devotion in the corresponding revelation, hero worship, or absolute trust in the leader" and "complete personal devotion" (p. 242). Charismatic authority, unlike bureaucratic authority, is in opposition to the rational: logic and rules, and overlaps strongly with populism.

Although they have countless significant differences, President Donald Trump and President Vladimir Putin both rule with such charismatic authority. The public refers to them in religious language, with Trump and Putin each being called a "savior" (Perper 2019; Robinson 2018) and "emperor" (Grove 2018), and considers them to be superhuman with unique extra-political powers that will lead their nation forward to revive its "greatness". Hence, as they are able to shape electoral outcomes and to guarantee the election success of their respective parties, their *leader effects* are strong.

Trump rallies are an excellent ethnographic space to observe the power of charismatic authority leading to unreflective emotional enthusiasm. Although during his rallies, he often makes false statements (at one campaign rally in Montana, 76% of his claims were false, misleading, or lacking evidence (Rizzo & Kelly 2018)), nevertheless his supporters continue to adore him (Rubin 2019). For example, Trump's slogan "Make America Great Again" has gone viral although few know what it means. His supporters, many of whom are emotionally-driven low-information voters (Fording & Schram 2017), find him personally-appealing, entertaining, and his message refreshingly-nostalgic, comforting, and encouraging (Petroski 2018).

Trump's leadership style has many commonalities with charismatic and cult leadership. Both styles of leadership overlap and tend to authoritarianism, bullying, coercion, need for regular enchantment, praise, and worship, and an absolute intolerance for criticism. Referencing sociologist Janja Lalich, a cult and charisma specialist, Jacobs (2018) writes that Trump's behavior and language on his base is characterized by an almost religious fervor, regular ridicule and chastising of 'the other', and ostracization of those who don't readily demonstrate *worship*. Trump's rally attendants adore relating to him with unreflective enchantment, feeling that by virtue of being in the presence of someone 'very special' they are superior and elite.

In line with populism which "polarizes the electorate into exclusionary groups" (Liddiard 2019), there is a huge emphasis on the binary seperation between 'us' and 'them'. This differentiation and separation from others is particularly characteristic of cults. Invoking this sense of specialness is both a recruitment and happiness strategy for its core. Confrontation and criticism remain rare. Janja Lalich, referencing Trump's supporters, states (as quoted by Jacobs 2018):

> absolutely kowtow to him.... It's about how people respond to that person, and how that person takes advantage of that.... We've all seen the videos of his aides praising him to high heaven. That's the kind of adulation cult leaders expect and demand.

She emphasizes that paranoia and fear-mongering of the 'other' and associating safety with Trump, characterizes his strategy. His charismatic strategy of invoking unreflective emotional fervor is so powerful, that some *believers* continue to support him, irrespective of his political merit. Trump is aware of his 'power' and infamously claimed: "I could stand in the middle of Fifth Avenue and shoot somebody and I wouldn't lose any voters" (Aratani 2019). Generating such unshakeable fervor and worship, for his persona, is reflective of Weber's charismatic authority.

Charismatic authority is more common and far more consequential in countries with limited liberal democracy, which run like dictatorships, and where elections are rigged, such as in Russia. Putin has been President since 2000, with a five-year break as Prime Minister, and plans to extend his presidency, possibly for life (Troianovski 2020). He remains popular (80% approval rating) and is known for the slogan "Strong President, Strong Russia" (Bennetts 2018). Although he runs his nation like a violent totalitarian regime, characterized by systemic corruption and stark inequality, with few opportunities for the average citizen, *Putinmania* has spread across Russia. Unreflectively, Russians adore him. There are numerous art exhibitions such as "Super Putin" (Porter 2017) and "Putin Universe", promoting his superhuman status (Standish 2015). The journalist Bennetts (2018) emphasizes that the internet is quilted with video appeals by ordinary Russians addressing Putin, referencing him by the familiar 'you' [*ty*] which is used with God and the Czar, and begging him to 'help' solve their troubles, such as unpaid government salaries. They always tiptoe around the issue of blame, even in clear cases of government abuse and negligence.

Such videos make religious references to his Godly image. Their sentiment is echoed in news reports which promote stories of Putin's generosity with poor children, referring to him as being responsible for 'everything' and 'embodying everything good'. In fact, many consider him the single and sole arbiter of Russian authority. The general sentiment that 'without Putin there is no Russia' is explicitly verbalized by politicians (*The Moscow Times* 2014). Bennetts (2018) emphasizes:

> Unlike in Western countries, where politicians are seen mostly as ordinary people, for millions of Russians, Putin is the living, breathing embodiment of the country. Which is why criticism of the 'national leader' is frequently interpreted as criticism of Mother Russia.

A pro-Kremlin genre of pop-culture songs also cultivate such a reification, referencing Putin as a best friend, 'cool', a superhero (Standish 2015), and strong

(Yelin 2002). Interestingly, such a pro-government genre is missing from the Anglo national pop-culture scene.

Pro-Kremlin artists promote a cult of personality, often including Putin's image in murals and portraits and depicting him as a Roman emperor, Alexander the Great, and Hercules, amongst other powerful characters (Standish 2015). For example, during Putin's first term, a female pop duo called Singing Together promoted Putin's cult of personality by scoring a hit with a viral song called *A Man Like Putin* (translated and adapted from Yelin 2002). Its chorus markets Putin as an ideal Russian man, contrasting him with regular men. This song includes the following romantic lyrics: "I want a man like Putin, who's full of strength. I want a man like Putin, who doesn't drink. I want a man like Putin, who won't make me sad. I want a man like Putin, who won't run away". This nationally-popular song went globally viral and as an apparent warning to President Trump, generated a parody remake by TV show host John Oliver (Shepherd 2017). Another song, by the rapper Timati, titled *My Best Friend* includes the lyrics: "My best friend is President Putin … the whole country is behind him, you know he's an awesome superhero" (Standish 2015). Why would Russians *after* the fall of the iron curtain, when offered democracy and liberalism, return to old ways, and continue to promote Putin's tyrannical rule?

Such attraction is mysterious and requires unpacking. According to my findings, Russians are avoiding anomie and boredom by remaining committed to their current political structure and charismatic President. Although, Putin's influence on their country is highly problematic, he's *their* president, and he's a continuation of the only system and style of rule that they have known. Hence, the current leadership meets the masses' needs of romanticizing the past, promoting familiarity, predictability, and strong central rule, all of which buffer anomie.

Is there a relationship between having a routine job and attraction to charismatic rule? In line with Sergey Brin's (Bokhari 2018) suggestion at the top of this chapter, Frey, Berger, and Chen (2017)[5] found that working a routine job positively correlated with voting for Trump in the 2016 election. They define routine jobs as "occupations mainly consisting of tasks following well-defined procedures that can easily be automated" (p. 2). Importantly, as long as the participant worked a routine job, *education level made no difference in the tendency to vote for Trump*. This finding suggests that experiencing daily redundancy (and likely, boredom) is more significant in influencing political decisions than higher education, especially as related to voting for charismatic leaders.

Frey, Berger, and Chen (2017) explain this trend vis-à-vis the 'politics of automation' or the fear of automation and jobs being replaced with machines. However, they fail to cite evidence for their explanation. An alternative explanation is that those in routine jobs experience daily chronic boredom and are drawn to Trump for his charismatic, comforting, and entertaining qualities. Importantly, their boredom may be of the simple common variety. Further investigation would allow us to fully unpack voters' particular experience.

Before Trump's election, Americans' confidence in Congress hovered at approximately 13–20% (Gallup 2016) and currently many Democrats are unhappy with the selection of anti-Trump candidates (Green 2019). There is a general sentiment of politics, and its debates having become boring (Garber 2020; Hennely 2019; Sunkara 2019). Importantly, while the democratic political stage seems to have dulled, Trump's supporters experience him as 'fun to watch' and entertaining (Weiss 2019) which may encourage those bored with status quo politics to support Trump.

Collaterally, it is interesting to consider the role of surplus political information in driving electoral anomie. Unlike the time period prior to mass media and the internet, currently, the electorate has to process and make sense of overwhelming amounts of information when deciding their vote. Logically interpreting copious information is challenging, which may encourage the electorate to vote emotionally. To simplify their task, and to bypass the logically-complex analysis of countless variables, the electorate may vote based on loyalty to a party or ideology, or based on charismatic attraction to a candidate. Klapp (1986) writes:

> Boredom is but one thread in the tangled skein of whatever may be wrong with modern life; but I think it tells of loss of meaning from overloads of information that are dysfunctional either because of too much redundancy or too much noise. (p. 12)

Such redundancy and noise prove confusing to filter, and often lead to indecision, and to boredom with the political process.

Van Tilburg and Igou (2016) conducted a series of experiments artificially-inducing boredom to assess its relationship with political ideology. In their first experiment, with 97 participants, they found that the emotional state of boredom leads to extreme political orientations. In their second experiment, with 859 participants, they found that those who naturally tend to boredom (personality trait) "adhere to more extreme ends of a political spectrum compared with their less easily bored counterparts" (p. 687). And in their third experiment, with 300 participants, they concluded that those who tend to boredom are searching for meaning. The authors posit that boredom's existential qualities of searching for meaning lead to adhering to extreme political orientations. Van Tilburg and Igou (2016) emphasize: "Herein lies boredom's functionality: The unpleasant experience serves as a cue that redirects people's behaviors toward the pursuit of acts with greater significance" (p. 687) and "boredom, at least when elicited by situational characteristics (e.g. dull activities), spurs the search for ideas and activities that increase a sense of meaningfulness" (p. 688). Hence, devotional political action in response to charismatic authority is an antidote to boredom and feels meaningful.

Anomie and boredom as motivation for terrorism

> The bores, and the terrorists, are alike confessing to impotence. If realpolitik is all smoke and mirrors and supercynicism, then why not embrace marginality.
>
> Amis 2009

Charismatic authority may be generalized on the level of a political movement and emanate through the sensationalism of extremist jihadi organizations such as ISIS. Such 'terrorist' movements offer a fatal attraction for those who struggle with anomie, isolation, subjective non-belonging, and boredom, leading recruits to vehemence, assault, and brutality. Due to their anomic placement within their host society, diaspora communities remain especially at risk for recruitment. Richardson (2007) describes the necessary societal criteria for terrorism to thrive:

> Terrorism needs a sense of alienation from the status quo and a desire to change it. Terrorism needs conditions in which people feel unfairly treated and leaders to make sense of these conditions, to organize a group and make it effective. Terrorism needs an all-encompassing philosophy—a religion or secular ideology—to legitimize violent action, to win recruits to the cause. (p. 69)

Immigration, by its characteristic traits of abandoning one's homeland, displacement, entering an alien society, and culture shock, is an anomic process with few opportunities for full resolution, especially for involuntary migrants who may remain 'existentially homeless' (Madison 2009). This experience is further shaped by the inherited brutal colonial legacy of many migrants (Hoffman 2017). Immigration leads to a redefinition of one's identity in relation to one's new host culture. Due to the host culture's difference, there is a huge vulnerability for developing a sense of non-belonging both socially and professionally and struggling with meaningful integration. Hence, immigration is a psychologically complex and burdensome process which amplifies anomie. Many succumb to its risks of marginalization, lack of meaningful occupation, resentment, and boredom (Atran 2010).

Critically, most foreign recruits to ISIS are Western European nationals who are radicalized due to a chronic state of non-belonging, including within the professional realm (Gouda and Marktanner 2018). They are unemployed and unoccupied until they discover extremist community which offers them a sense of belonging, a clear and 'highly valued' role, and salary. In Amis's (2009) conception, as outlined in the quote at the beginning of this section, recruits embrace their marginality. Atran (2010) and Sageman (2008) found that being a new unemployed immigrant was a risk factor for attraction and participation in extremism as it offered an escape from "terrible boredom" (Atran 2010, p. 290). In their study titled, "Muslim Youth Unemployment and Expat Jihadism: Bored to Death?", Gouda and Marktanner (2018) write:

> Our results show that youth unemployment in both Muslim countries and among Muslims in Western countries is a strong predictor of expat jihadism. Youth unemployment among Muslims therefore serves as an early warning indicator, deserving of specific policy attention, regardless of the region.... Push factors include: estrangement by mainstream society of uprooted migrants in refugee camps and diasporas; socio-economic marginalization

and aggravation; relative depravation and/or political exclusion; lack of future prospects at home; and desire to escape. (pp. 879–881)

Gouda and Marktanner (2018) found a strong relationship between a nation's youth unemployment rate in Muslim countries, and its propensity for producing jihadi expat recruits to ISIS and for supplying Syria with foreign fighters. In an article titled "Terrorists' Most Powerful Recruiting Tool: Boredom", Power (2015) explains that the boredom of the unemployed leads to radicalization:

> a key recruiting tool for violent jihadis: boredom.... For young people in Yemen, where youth unemployment is about 50%, the possibilities of ordinary life must pale besides joining a transnational band to fight in a foreign land.

Leaders of extremism understand the vulnerabilities of alienated, confused, and unoccupied youth, and strategically target them (Callimachi 2015), further isolating them from their host society while translating their struggle into the language of holy war (Power 2015).

Although extremist jihadi movements often criticize modernity and the trappings of technology (Berman 2004), their recruitment is high tech and they maintain a huge presence online across multiple social media platforms (Hoffman 2017). Specifically, recruitment occurs online through YouTube and other social platforms which offer curated jihadi videos for those raised on Western pop culture that simulate video games and snowboarding videos and reference Disney characters (Power 2015), cleverly bridging extremism with mainstream popular culture. Speaking to Westerner's alienation, boredom, and utilizing familiar cultural references, these videos promise brotherhood, sisterhood, and community. Stern (2003) writes:

> cult leaders can harness alienation and anomie to construct a group identity, eventually creating killers out of lost souls. (p. 30)
> [...]
> Lone-wolf are often inspired by strains of anomie ... they may sympathize with the grievances expressed by particular terrorist movements. (p. 171)

While recruits to terrorism are often in transition, unable to manage their freedom, and feeling alienated, anomic, and bored, the movements' leadership harnesses these difficulties for their agenda.

This draws young westerners to terrorist organizations such as al-Qaeda and ISIS, not for Islam per se, but for the sense of meaningful purpose it provides. Haque et al. (2015) discuss their findings:

> [w]hat could possibly compel otherwise financially stable young Westerners (non-Muslim as well as Muslim) to leave their families, friends, and home culture, and take up an uncertain future by joining a terrorist organization

like ISIS?... One way to summarize our answer is that as an ideology, ISIS provides existential fast food, and for some of the most spiritually hungry young Westerners, ISIS is like a Big Mac amidst a barren wasteland of an existence.... Who actually joins ISIS? Not psychopaths or the brainwashed, but rather everyday young people in social transition, on the margins of society, or amidst a crisis of identity.... For the most part they have no traditional religious education and are "born again" to religion.... For lonely young people in transition, ISIS provides a quick fix to the perennial problems of human life.... Specifically, the relief in question concerns the human desire for identity, certainty, social connection, meaning, the optimal amount of freedom, and glory.... For youths on the margins of Western society, and in transition from one community to the next, this process of identity formation can become a hopeless task. When one has become a fringe member of one's home community in America during crucial phases of identity formation, it is very tempting to join what appears to be a righteous struggle against one's oppressive community.... Whatever its factual merits, a pluralistic worldview denies its adherents the delights of absolute certainty, and it takes much cognitive effort to maintain. ISIS provides an ideology in which the world is divided into absolute good and evil, no compromises are possible, radical Islam is the solution to all human problems, and any other interpretation of Islam is unthinkable. Why settle for shades of grey in a messy world when "The Truth" is packaged and delivered in under 30 seconds via Internet sound bites?... It can provide epistemological crème brûlée for drifting and unanchored Western youths.... **ISIS presents to the bored, secure, and the uninspired in Western liberal democracies a thrilling cause and call to action that promises glory and esteem in the eyes of friends.**

Prior to joining ISIS and other jihadi movements, their lives felt subjectively boring. Importantly, they may have been attracted to other ideological movements such as cults.

Stern (2003) describes the perspective of English terrorist Ahmed Omar Saeed Sheikh who was known as 'Osama Bin Laden's special son' and connected to the September 11 hijackers and to al-Qaeda:

> [He] was born in 1973 to an upper-middle-class family of Pakistani immigrants living in the U.K. He attended elite private schools ... his teachers considered him a model student. But he was apparently unhappy and frequently got into fights ... the students at his school were racist and taunted him.... He returned to England to attend the London School of Economics in 1992 ... but quit, apparently bored, in his second year of college.... He made contact with Pakistani jihadi groups. (p. 196)

After hearing their experiences, Sheikh joined a jihadi group and continued with military training. He took assignments which included orchestrating kidnappings of Westerners and raising money for the recruitment of new members and for jihad operations, and most notably is infamous for beheading of Wall Street Journal reporter Daniel Pearl.

Boredom and war

Even though most of us associate war with horror, atrocity, and senseless casualties, Hitler romanticized serving in the frontlines of WWI as the greatest time of his life (Kustermans and Ringmar 2011). It offered him camaraderie and meaningful heroism. Kustermans and Ringmar (2011, p. 1788) write: "What Hitler hated was everything he believed to stand in the way of such dynamism. The aim of the Nazi Party after 1933 was to replicate the ethos of the trenches on a national, indeed a Pan-European, level". They continue to explain the relationship between charismatic rule and violence: "Death, indiscriminately administered by a superhero, makes us feel good about ourselves. And the more boring our existence, the more urgent the demand for such mediatized violence" (p. 1789). As discussed above, people are unreflectively drawn to charismatic authority and 'superhero' leaders because it makes them feel good. Connecting to such authority, directly and vicariously, offers them unlimited agency. Sometimes such agency includes committing cruel acts of violence. Kustermans and Ringmar (2011) elaborate:

> To torture another human being is the ultimate transgressive act; torture is also the ultimate affirmation of one's agency. Suddenly, you have all the power and the person subject to you has none.... Torture, just as terrorism, is the ultimate antidote to boredom. (p. 1790)

Accounts of war and violence relieving boredom, demonstrate that in fact, war and violence relieve anomie by offering purpose and confidence combined with overpowering sensory stimulation.

In another example, Hannah Arendt ([1963] 2006), in applying her concept of the *banality of evil*, posits that Adolf Eichmann applied to join the Schutzstaffel (S. S.) not out of an ideological sentiment and hatred for Jews, but out of boredom with his professional life, which consisted of working as a traveling salesman and being an officer and corporal in the military. In *Eichmann in Jerusalem: A Report on the Banality of Evil* ([1963] 2006) she explains:

> he did not enter the Party out of conviction, nor was he ever convinced by it—whenever he was asked to give his reasons, he repeated the same embarrassed clichés about the Treaty of Versailles and unemployment; rather as he pointed out in court, "it was like being swallowed up by the Party against all expectations and without previous decision. It happened so quickly and suddenly". He had no time and less desire to be properly informed, he did not even know the Party program, he never read *Mein Kampf*. Kaltenbrunner said to him: Why not join the S.S.? And he had

replied: Why not? That was how it had happened.... What Eichmann failed to tell the presiding judge in cross-examination was that he had been an ambitious young man who was fed up with his job as a traveling sales man. ... From a humdrum life without significance and consequence the wind had blown him into History ... into a Movement that always kept moving and in which somebody like him—already a failure in the eyes of his social class, of his family, and hence in his own eyes as well—could start from scratch and still make a career ... he might still have preferred—if anybody had asked him—to be hanged as *Obersturmbannführer a.D.* (in retirement) rather than living out his life quietly and normally as a traveling salesman. (pp. 33–34)

After his traveling sales job, Eichmann joined the military and found it boring as well, and out of this boredom eventually joined the S.S. Arendt (2006) quotes Eichmann's reflection: "The humdrum of military service, that was something I couldn't stand, day after day always the same" (p. 35). She explains "Thus bored to distraction, he heard that the Security Service of the Reichsführer S.S. ... had jobs open and applied immediately" (p. 35). Hence, Arendt suggests that Eichmann, along with other S.S. officers, chose a career of cruelty, torture, and murder over a life of mediocrity and boredom.

Historian Michael Howard (2000) in *Invention of Peace* posits that modern society causes boredom while war provides an antidote as well as an excellent outlet for those bored:

There is something about rational order that will always leave some people, especially the energetic young, deeply and perhaps rightly dissatisfied.... Militant nationalist movements or conspiratorial radical ones provide excellent outlets for boredom. In combination, their attraction can prove irresistible. (p. 12)

In fact, war is a way of restoring agency and capacity. And the societal mood of boredom can encourage the public to support war efforts. Rose (1965, p. 102 as quoted in McDonough 2017) writes: "There is one theory which holds that wars start when people are bored. In our particular historical situation, without the threat of famine or plague, it should not be surprising that boredom should be a common experience". A huge breadth of literature establishing that boredom characterizes the experience of soldiers and military personnel during war (Laugesen 2012; Kustermans and Kingmar 2011; Maeland and Brunstad 2009; Terrence 1982).

Additionally, it is interesting to consider the power to impose boredom as a mechanism of social control and the way it was enacted by dictatorships such as the Soviet Union. In his Pulitzer Prize winning novel *Humboldt's Gift* ([1975] 2008, p. 200), Saul Bellow writes: "an instrument of social control. Power is the power to impose boredom, to command stasis, to combine this stasis with anguish. The real tedium, deep tedium, is seasoned with terror and with death". He suggests that when the imposition of boredom is combined with terror, existential boredom results. Hence, different structural systems result in different styles of boredom, and the Soviet type was deliberately cultivated in the masses as a form of enforced powerlessness and social control. Bellow ([1975] 2008) describes boredom generally within the S.U. as well as during Stalin's dinners:

> the most boring society in history. Dowdiness shabbiness dullness dull goods boring buildings discomfort boring supervision a dull press dull education boring bureaucracy forced labour perpetual police presence penal presence, boring party congresses, et cetera. What was permanent was the defeat of interest.... What could be more boring than the long dinners Stalin gave, as Djilas describes them? Even I, a person seasoned in boredom by my years in Chicago, marinated, *mithridated* by the USA, was horrified by Djilas's account of those twelve-course all-night banquets. The guests drank and ate, and ate and drank, and then at 2 a.m. they had to sit down to watch an American Western. Their bottoms ached. There was dread in their hearts. Stalin, as he chatted and joked, was mentally picking those who were going to get it in the neck and while they chewed and snorted and guzzled they knew this, they expected shortly to be shot.... This combination of power and boredom has never been properly examined. Boredom is an instrument of social control. Power is the power to impose boredom, to command stasis, to combine this stasis with anguish. The real tedium, deep tedium, is seasoned with terror and with death.

Stalin may in fact have deliberately implemented boredom for power as well as to test the loyalty of his subjects. As Soviet society was not only boring but challenging to survive and deeply fear-inducing, citizens were often confused about the rules of conduct and found themselves stuck in paralyzing fear (Balagov 2019). Bellow ([1975] 2008) provides an example: Stalin's dinner guests submissively resigned themselves to sitting and listening to him for hours, and self-consciously responded to the best of their ability, aware that one wrong word could result in their assassination. These guests were prominent members of the 'polit bureau' and knew their social role well—yet Stalin's power allowed him to decide their fate. They serve as the archetypal example for the Russian style of boredom: they knew themselves well yet society was not comfortably befitting, even to the point of terror, and death.

Indifference as political activism

Indifference can be a powerful political stance as one neither agrees nor disagrees, and by abstaining from opinion, protects oneself from persecution for their 'otherness'. In the 1950s, post WWII, and during the highly policed society of the Cold War, many intellectuals enacted an attitude of indifference to obfuscate and obscure their otherness and stay invincible. By opting out of direct political participation, they may have resisted and destabilized the dominant hegemony which depends on a binary dynamic of support versus opposition (in the form of an 'other') to function. Roth (Roth and Katz 2013) writes:

The 1950s were assaulted with literature, popular culture and art describing feelings of indifference, neutrality and passivity in the world of the Cold War ... in the early 1950s, a growing number of intellectuals consciously espoused indifference as a virtue, as the correct way to deal with an uncertain world. (p. 34)

Instead of strongly investing in a political agenda and opening oneself to personal disappointment and external attack, many intellectuals protected themselves by maintaining a stance of 'no opinion'. Queer intellectuals and artists of the 1950s were well-documented for such a stance (Peiss, Simmons, & Padgug 1989). During this period, homosexuality was considered a mental illness and moral perversion, denunciations were common. There was a politically-driven witch hunt on those thought to be homosexuals, and fear was high. By virtue of being queer, they faced discrimination, attack, and death threats. Assuming a political stance could have sabotaged their professional advancement and further exposed Queer intellectuals to danger. In response to a homophobic political and social climate, they assumed a conflict-averse stance of indifference (Peiss, Simmons, & Padgug 1989). Delicately negotiating self-disclosure in this manner meant survival. In such a context, the gay musical composer John Cage in his *Lecture on Nothing* openly declared: "I have nothing to say and I'm saying it" (Cage 1973, p. 210). Such high-profile slogans were a subtle way of shifting the tone of anomie into an empowered and decisive "No opinion".

This case is interesting to consider from the perspective of Durkheim's theory of surplus regulation or fatalism. It appears that Cold War American society heavily policed social norms and punished those who mis-stepped. For the Queer community who held a strong and powerful identity and felt a deep self-knowing regarding their sexuality and sexual practices, such restriction felt both suffocating and life-threatening. As they were unsafe to unabashedly 'be themselves', they resorted to the 'boring' politics of no opinion. Yet, anomie could lead to this case as well. Let us consider that queer artists, overwhelmed by the greater anomic cultural atmosphere and countless identity options (in addition, they could have emphasized other characteristics of their persona besides being queer and an artist), felt overwhelmed by anomie and chose to focus on their Queer identity as a way of simplifying their life. Hence, this could serve as a mixed case, where surplus regulation in terms of identity led to fear-based political absenteeism and inadequate regulation led to a strong commitment to Queer artist identity at the exclusion of other identity characteristics. This phenomenon of strong identity commitment is ubiquitous and applies to most identities in free society. As it is easy to be overwhelmed by countless political choices, a common reaction to information-overload is strong identity and ideological commitment, even if that commitment is to 'indifference'. Hence, those invoking a strategy of 'no opinion' were so overwhelmed by the informational anomie of conflicting opinions (Klapp 1986) that they chose to simplify their life and their political image by opting out. Theoretically, they could have strained and made an effort to introspect their personal opinion but found this dangerous, and potentially, too burdensome an effort.

Notes

1 Video posted by Bokhari (2018).
2 Quoted text of David Carnegie is from: Mrs. Robert Moss [August E.] King, The Diary of a Civilian's Wife in India, 1877–1882 (London: Richard Bentley & Son, 1994), 261.
3 Ibid.
4 As referenced in Marryat (1868)
5 This study surveyed 3,108 counties and plotted the percentage share of routine jobs in each respective county alongside the percentage of people in that county who voted for Trump, demonstrating a significant positive relationship.

5   Notes on anomie

Including portraits of the bored

This chapter presents additional cases for anomie being the cause of boredom. In an environment with extended temporality such as waiting in line or for friends to arrive at a party, an individual with adequate scripts (mental and behavioral), will not experience boredom. Boredom can only result as an extension of anomie, with temporality being an important secondary characteristic increasing the likelihood of the development of boredom and its emotional intensity. Temporality, as a single variable without anomie, fails to lead to boredom. Every social institution and experience offers a temporal structure/rhythm, which may amplify stability and predictability, or disorganization, confusion, and boredom. Importantly, having a present, versus a past or a future focus, is an essential characteristic of experiencing boredom. Yet, present-focus, on its own, fails to cause boredom. One may experience being pleasantly in the moment, as when enjoying gazing at the stars or meditating. However, one cannot experience boredom without being in the moment. To emphasize, those focused on the past or future, cannot experience boredom. This chapter will present case studies that illuminate these nuances.

The Anglo case

Sociology is predicated on the influence of social conditions on humanity's subjective experience. I argue that conditions of excess: unorganized time and leisure, coupled with the decline of tradition, in both Anglo and Russian society, created an anomic crisis of meaning leading to boredom. Although most research, whether biologically or sociologically-oriented, focuses on boredom driven by lack: the boredom of isolation, solitary confinement, sensory deprivation, Klapp (1986) emphasizes that modern society is an *information society* which inundates us with surplus information which is impossible to meaningfully process and integrate: "boredom as we experience it today is more likely to be from an *overload* than an underload" (p. 3). Since the information and internet revolution, researchers have begun considering the consequences of sensory overload (Simmel 1950; Miller 1960; Deutsch 1961; Meier 1962; Klapp 1986; Belton 2016). This phenomenon creates a mental traffic-jam, making it difficult for us to distill and consolidate information rationally and meaningfully. Such information-chaos is inherently anomic, and as we are lost swimming in an ocean of unmanageable, unorganized, and confusing content, leads to boredom.

As discussed throughout this study, modern society is anomic, facing a crisis of meaning, yet biased towards radical freedom and anomie. Its foundational belief systems have atrophied and become precarious and have yet to be replaced with another solid foundation. Most Westerners no longer know what they believe and continue in an endless search of self-discovery. We are infiltrated with endless volumes of content on competing ways of being, competing experiences, competing choices from which most of us are in a near-constant state of anomic mental chaos. The signal to noise ratio is low (Shannon and Weaver 1949). Klapp (1986) elaborates:

> Along with all this information came a less comfortable feeling that it was not making more sense—even with the help of computers – than it had before. The **modern world was in a crisis of meaning**, that one need only mention names like Kafka, Sartre, Beckett, and Eliot to demonstrate. The crisis has been called by many names—alienation, existential despair, absurdity, disenchantment, legitimation crisis, identity problems, **anomie**, sensate culture, counterculture, future shock, end of ideology, false consciousness, to mention a few.... In a crisis of meaning, amidst all the facts, one finds little by way of conviction that is reliable to hang onto. Traditions are discarded, institutions—even the most hallowed—are weakly legitimated ... **people are continually on the verge of boredom because so much information is irrelevant, meaningless, or trivial**—or urgent but they can do nothing about it. We see boredom as having a defensive function as a barrier against noise. What such negative elements in the appetite for information suggest is that along with the growth of information there has been a decline in its marginal value or meaning ... another useful economic analogy is that the decline of value of information was rather like an inflation of currency: the more there was of it, the less it seemed to 'buy' in meaning. (pp. 8–9)

We can only receive useful information and answers if we are deliberate in consuming information and seeking the right questions. In modernity, we are subsumed by a deluge of senseless data, which is personally meaningless, hence boring. This informationally-anomic atmosphere is the breeding ground for boredom.

Different types of anomie emerge in Anglo and Russian society and their differences spark the emergence of different affective experiences of boredom. These two societies shaped two different expressions of social deficiency. Within the breadth of literature on boredom in the Anglo world, we find regular mention of distraction as a defense mechanism against boredom. This is significant as it underlines the major distinction between its Anglo and Russian varieties. As mentioned in the Introduction chapter, Anglo boredom results from an inadequate completion of the identity process. As having a clear identity is essential in human society, not knowing oneself results in psychological discomfort and suffering. Distraction is enacted to protect against the discomfort of boredom. *Distraction is a level above boredom. Distraction masks boredom.* If people stop distracting themselves, they will become bored. And the reason they are constantly distracting themselves is because of *the fear that characterizes boredom*: if they were to become bored, they would not be able to come up with something to do. It has become ubiquitous and fueled countless industries and activities: from entertainment such as movies, gambling, and video games to adrenaline sports and drug-seeking.

Table 5.1 Portrait of Anglo distraction

Distraction is like a person sitting in his room binge watching Netflix afraid of a potential moment of silence during which time boredom could set in, and he wouldn't know what else to do. His binge watching is driven by the fear of anomie. Whereas someone who was more sure of himself, could sit in silence and allow himself to be bored knowing that eventually he will come up with something subjectively interesting to do, that is intrinsic to himself.

This fear is an extension of an insecure identity. Any activity—including intellectual pursuit, eating, or lovemaking, if used as a distraction—exists to avoid boredom. Distraction can be thought of as treading water to avoid the sinking of boredom. One will do anything to avoid sinking as one will generally do anything to avoid boredom. The fact that distraction exists as a common defense mechanism supports the observation that boredom is a common social ill. The incredible amount of distraction and distraction-led activities in modern society, especially in the information age (Klapp 1986), speaks to its spread and ubiquity.

As discussed previously, many would rather experience pain than sit still with their own thoughts. This is a horrifying predicament and in line with research on boredom-driven violence such as hooliganism, bullying, gang activity, as well as other violent crime (Kustermans and Ringmar 2011; Arendt [1963] 2006; Klapp 1986). These may be considered as "crimes committed against boredom itself" as well as "larger efflorescences of political and cultural rebellion" (Ferrell 2004, p. 287). Klapp (1986) writes:

> Some people are trapped in boring jobs or situations. Some boredom may be in the eye of the beholder. Some is due to social structure or culture that affects many, though participation varies.… A strange cloud hangs over modern life.… It embarrasses claims that the quality of life is getting better. … It is thickest in cities where there are the most varieties, pleasures, and opportunities.… The most common name for this cloud is boredom. And the most common mistake is to think of it as occurring only in monotonous work and the long traffic-jammed rides. (p. 11)

The current epidemic of boredom opposes the common view that society is improving and progressing. In fact, many contemporary social ills such as crime, violence, and substance abuse result from boredom:

Boredom, at the very least, helps breed some of America's uglier social trends. The rate of teenage suicide has more than tripled in the United States since 1955, and psychiatrists across the country lay part of the blame to boredom born of unrealistic expectations and frustration. Divorce condemns nearly half of all marriages, and marriage counselors report boredom as a major cause. Drug and alcohol abuse—which has increased more rapidly in the past decade among middle- and upper-class teen-agers than among the less wealthy—is caused, in part, by the need to kill time (Student 1982). Boredom is a factor for shoplifters, many of whom can afford to buy what they steal; ... for housewives who besiege doctors with mystery ailments and undergo unnecessary hysterectomies that give them the kind of attention and legitimacy that complaints about boredom cannot (Harden 1982).

Hence, although we insist that society is progressing, unless we resolve boredom, old problems will be replaced by new problems.

I posit that *boredom is caused by and further fuels anomie*. It creates a cyclical feed-back loop which wreaks havoc on one's social structure and stability. *Boredom is caused by anomie and if unresolved, as it fails to offer structural direction, becomes a condition for maintaining anomie.* In order for a society to exist, its members need to reify their belief in that society by maintaining it with regular participation. If belief in society is lost, so is its social role maintenance. Framed differently, if we develop boredom with our society and with our social role, society may decline and end. In fact, *Anglo traditions, such as marriage and religious participation, may be declining because we are too bored to uphold them.* Klapp (1986, p. 3) quotes Boulding (1976) on this point: "Because boredom signals fading interest, it means a loss of human potential, for a certain line of action at least; and loss of potential is one definition of entropy". Klapp (1986) elaborates (p. 3): "By-products of boredom, such as low morale, thrill seeking, gambling, drug abuse, vandalism, and crime are loss of potential ... increasing entropy of modern society in spite—and to some extent on account—of its large information load". If we apply his analysis to loss of faith in institution and ritual, we may conclude that the contemporary person has a hard time buying into the values and rituals of traditional institutions due to countless competing belief systems. This leads to anomie (disorientation) and contributes to mass scale entropy. Another perspective to consider, reminiscent of Weber's concept of the iron cage, is that we may simply be too bored to uphold tradition, because it has lost its magic for us, no longer believing in its power of connection to the divine, to society, and to our close ones. With declining perso-nal and social engagement, the foundation of our society is undermined, fueling intense anomie.

Table 5.2 Portrait of Anglo boredom

Boredom is like a person without internet sitting in his room wondering what he's going to do. He knows that he'll eventually do something so he's *anticipating what* he's going to do. Yet, while he's in his room and pondering, he's experiencing anomie and feels bored.

Boredom and work

Work and maintaining busyness are central to American culture. Americans identify strongly with their work, profession, and with staying occupied. However, in modern society, most jobs have become routine, repetitive, predictable, and redundant, and people find themselves busy yet bored. Unfortunately for many, associating work with boredom begins in adolescence. Krasko (2004) explains:

> We encourage children to work and as early as possible. By so doing we make them take the first steps toward existential misery in the future. Too early do they learn that a job is *boring*, adding to the general boredom of their everyday meaningless lives. They then try to escape this boredom through entertainment, promiscuous sex, and drugs. The notion that any job that brings in money is good (and the more money the better) is profoundly wrong. A job is good if it brings satisfaction. With satisfaction comes happiness. (p. xxii)

If we have a job that is not satisfying, we remain maladjusted, as our identity does not fit neatly with our environment, creating discomfort and boredom. Millennials are twice as likely as baby boomers to find their work boring (Udemy Team 2016).

A British, human resources consulting firm found that one third of Britons were bored for most of the day while half who worked in finance were bored either 'often' or 'always' (DDI 2004). Klapp (1986) describes work, in America, also as boring:

To be sure, work is much to blame.... National magazines periodically run stories with captions like, "Bored on the job (Life)", or "Boredom Epidemic—Illness of the Age" (National Observer, May 13, 1972). Work is described in terms like the following: "The women may not even know what they are assembling or who will use it. They are bored.... Practically every survey of attitudes toward work reveals boredom, especially where work is monotonous, mechanized, and control is lacking over the whole task. A task force of the Department of Health, Education, and Welfare (HEW) in 1972 issued a massive report on "Work in America", declaring that the American work force was becoming dissatisfied with dull, unchallenging, and repetitive jobs. (p. 12)

For monotonous tasks to feel satisfying, they have to be approached with personal meaning, importance, and as an extension of one's identity, or as a contemplative spiritual practice, similar to repetitive prayer in the Christian tradition or to meditation in the Eastern tradition.

Research establishes that white collar jobs can also be boring. Harju and Hakanen (2016) interviewed 72 employees in white collar jobs and delimited three types of work-related boredom:

1   Inertia at work which is characterized by a 'stagnant present' caused by person-job misfit, routinization, and idleness.

2 Acceleration at work which is characterized by overactivation and over-stimulation caused by work overload, a rapid pace, hectic conditions, and unrealistic goals.
3 Dysrhythmia at work characterized by regular distraction and inefficiency caused by constraint and problematic cooperation.

These three types serve as supporting cases for my theory. The first type of boredom, inertia, occurs when one's job fails to offer future-oriented goals and a sense of progress. Such jobs are monotonous and routinized with minimal space for personal creativity and innovation, leaving one in a directionless 'stagnant present'. In this case, one's boredom is driven by a focus on an unsatisfying present. The second and third types, acceleration at work and dysrhythmia, are both caused by an anomic environment that is overstimulating and hectic in the former case, and distracting and non-cooperative in the latter case.

Furthermore, the acronym of 'TGIF': 'Thank God it's Friday', and the idioms of 'the daily grind' and 'hump day' and the neologism of *boredom room* and *boreout* signal the ubiquitous boredom of the American workplace. *Boredom room* (or *banishment room*) is an employee exit management strategy in which unwanted employees are transferred to another department and given meaningless tasks until their boredom and frustration pressures them to voluntarily resign, losing eligibility for benefits (Tabuchi 2013). Many experience it as a type of purgatory of waiting for nothingness.

While boreout, first identified in 2007, refers to boredom boreout syndrome: a psychological disorder of boredom, stress, fatigue, low-confidence, and frustration, driven by a mismatch between one's mental capacity and professionally meaningful tasks, leading to physical illness and suicide risk (Rothlin and Werder 2008). This concept is composed of two stems, with 'out' emphasizing having reached the limits of boredom (p. 7). This phenomenon is the opposite of burnout in that it is characterized by inadequate challenge (p. 10). It speaks to anomie in the workplace, a lack of organized/meaningful activity, and its consequence of chronic boredom (Rothlin and Werder 2008). For developing boreout, lack of subjectively meaningful work tasks are more consequential than lack of stress. Office jobs pose the greatest risk.

Frankfurt psychotherapist, Wolfgang Merkle, describes the phenomenon as similar to burnout in its consequences: it leads to depression, anxiety, headaches, dizziness, ulcers, and cardiovascular disease amongst other symptoms (Uchtmann 2012). Verifying boreout, a British study titled "Bored to Death?" discovered that experiencing chronic boredom at work (*workplace ennui*) is bad for health and correlates with younger death (Britton and Shipley 2010). Referencing Sommers and Vodanovih (2000), they write: "the state of boredom is almost certainly a proxy for other risk factors ... proneness to boredom, particularly in younger populations, could be indicative of harmful behaviours such as excessive drinking, smoking, taking drugs and low psychological profiles" (p. 371). Rothlin and Werder (2008) emphasize that boreout is common and widespread.

Workplace boredom is ubiquitous. A 2017 study of workplace boredom by Office Team, a staffing firm, found that employees were bored approximately 10.5 hours per week (O'Bannon 2017). Males and those between the "ages of 28 and 34 were bored more often for 12 and 14 hours, respectively" (p. 18). Boredom was found to negatively correlate with productivity, due to withdrawal from one's environment and subsequently reduced cognitive engagement (Csikszentmihalyi 2000; Davies and Fortney 2012), often caused by a mismatch between one's ability and environmental challenge (Reijseger et al., 2013), subjectively experienced as low arousal and dissatisfaction (Mikulas and Vodanovich 1993). Countless studies, conducted since the 1970's, offer similar findings (Cummings, Gao, & Thornburg 2015; Mann 2007; Terkel 1973).

The Russian case

A few cases of boredom were recorded during the Soviet Era: the case of revolutionaries after 1917 (Figes 2008); the case of housewives during Stalinism who were sent to join their husband on developments projects in remote regions (Fitzpatrick 1999); the case of children orphaned during Stalinism and left to fend for themselves (Figes 2008); and artists participating in the Non-Conformist Movement (McDonough 2017; Narusyte 2010). As Soviet society was hugely regimented and challenging to survive, most did not take to boredom. After the Revolution, the work week was six days long, while for 11 years during Stalin's reign the continuous work week prevailed with rare days off (Frost 2018). Surviving outside of formal work also proved challenging. Housing was distributed by the government, and most lived with their parents and children in a one-room communal apartment, sharing one bathroom and kitchenette with dozens of neighbors. There were either no or few amenities such as electricity, running water, and appliances, with neither diapers nor washing machines. Acquiring water for drinking, washing, and cooking generally involved a walk to a well and a walk up a long flight of stairs or awaiting a special water delivery truck where each neighbor was allowed to fill a bucket for personal use. Women carried the double shift—expected to work full time and assume all child-rearing and domestic responsibilities (Fitzpatrick 1999). For the average *Homo Sovieticus*, [1] surviving was excruciatingly consuming to the point that there was almost no anomie and, by extension, almost no boredom.

However exceptional cases were documented. Those who believed and participated in the Russian Revolution were hugely disappointed after the installation of the Soviet Regime (Figes 2008). Bellow ([1975] 2008) juxtaposes Soviet boredom with its thrilling original promise of ongoing Trotskyite revolution and its dream of creating a utopian society. Following revolution, this promise resulted in a painful and often deadly disappointment. Survivors were left to the daily drudgery of monotonous grey reality. If Soviet propaganda had worked, people would be full with passion for building communism.

Russians participation in the Revolution was lured with promises of an 'ongoing revolution' that would conquer the world (later deemed impractical by Lenin and Stalin) and with promises of a utopian quality of life, the result of which became living in squalid close quarters with strangers, hard labor in the face of abject poverty, starvation, constant surveillance by the government, and under regular threat of terror and death. This gap between ideal and reality, especially affected revolutionaries who strongly identified with their role in creating a utopian society. Yet after the Revolution project, they had little left to do and were unsure of how to occupy themselves in a meaningful way. This created an anomic atmosphere which led to boredom. They experienced the Russian-style of boredom: revolutionaries had a clear identity with clear aspirations but society had no opportunities for their expression, which left them maladjusted and emotionally numb. Figes (2008, p. 73) quotes 1. a Stalinist and 2. a utopian artist and government museum director Aleksei Radchenko:

1   In the Komsomols [communist youth] of my generation—those who experienced the October Revolution at the age of ten or younger—chafed at our fate. In the Komsomol [Communist Youth Organization], in the factories, we lamented that there was nothing remaining for us to do: the Revolution was over, the harsh but romantic years of the Civil War would not come again, and the older generation had left us only a boring, prosaic life devoid of [revolutionary] struggle and excitement. (Year Unknown)
2   Progressive youth today has no real interest or focus for activity—these are not the years of the Civil War just the NEP [New Economic Policy]— a necessary stage of the Revolution but a boring one. People are distracted by personal affairs, by family matters.... We need something to shake us up and clear the air (some people even dream of war). (1927)

Additionally, many felt that the society they had fought and sacrificed to create was a sham, and referred to it as a giant work camp (Figes 2008). Revolutionaries knew themselves well-enough to assess that societal conditions were not a good match for the social role they wanted to play, leading to existential boredom.

Another rare case of anomie and boredom consisted of the predicament of housewives during Stalin's Reign (Fitzpatrick 1999). In the Soviet Union, women were 'emancipated' and were expected to contribute to the 'Great Communist Cause' via work. 'Wife' was not a reified category as Soviet women were discouraged from identifying with their husband and domesticity and were expected to associate closely with their "work and activity outside of the home" (Fitzpatrick 1999, p. 156). Since they did not fit the National ideal, Soviet housewives found themselves in an anomic situation: their status and contribution to the family were ignored and reproached. They became alienated from society and eventually from their husbands, who were actively participating in the Communist Cause and eventually began viewing their wives through the State Propaganda lens as ignorant and bad citizens.

According to propaganda, both men and women's responsibilities and potential contribution were identical, yet the double-shift was expected of women. Most Soviet women were very active professionally and professions from which women were blocked entry in the West—such as being a physician—were dominated by women. Housewives were seen as belonging to the dirty category of the bourgeois as they did not work directly for the State and contribute directly to the 'Great Communist Cause'; they were demoted to being second class citizens. Fitzpatrick (1999) quotes two housewives who clearly express their alienation:

1   Sometimes I thought that we housewives were not even considered human.
2   The more time [my husband] spent at the factory, the more he participated in construction, the larger was the distance between us. He made new acquaintances. They were not just engineers—industrial administrators and party workers began to frequent our house.... Ever since childhood I had been taught to entertain guests.... I remember the time when I was an expert at this art. But it turned out that this is not enough to be able to make conversation; one had to know what to talk about.... Once, as I was trying to carry on a conversation [with a Communist], I looked at my husband and stopped short. His eyes were full of anxiety and terrible pity. (pp. 156–157)

Housewives resented their inferior status and found themselves in generally anomic and boring life circumstances.

In the style of Russian boredom, they chose and wanted to be housewives yet their society admonished them for identity and life choices. Society degraded their persona and suppressed their capacity to openly and spontaneously express themselves. They could not be outspoken about their choice or pride of running their household, as this would expose them to criticism for not being good communists. Hence, they found themselves awfully bored in social situations.

Those sent to join their husband on developments projects in remote regions were even worse off as they were socially isolated with few amenities (Fitzpatrick 1999). He describes their letters and predicament:

they wrote feeling of emptiness of life ... when the only events were visiting the hairdresser and going to parties with the same guests, and nothing to talk about. Time hung heavy on the wives' hands, and they often quarreled with their husbands.... Wives from a pre-revolutionary intelligentsia background—as many of the engineers' wives still were—suffered particularly from the loneliness and lack of culture around them, all the more if their husbands developed close relationships with the Communists with whom they worked. (p. 157)

The more intellectual and culturally-rich their internal world, the more they struggled to connect with the new Soviet society. Their situation serves as an archetypal case for the Russian style of boredom: although they knew themselves, there was no appropriate social space to express their identity. In May 1936, with the instatement of The Wives Movement—which initiated and trained housewives to help with the communist cause—they found themselves socially occupied, and their predicament largely ended.

Another exceptional case of Soviet boredom is found in the phenomenon of abandoned children during the Stalinist Era. As part of the 'Reign of Terror', millions of parents were arrested, imprisoned, evacuated, murdered, or sent to the Gulag internment and concentration camp system. As a consequence, some of their children were abandoned to fend for themselves. Figes (2008) explains and provides an archetypal example:

> But the arrest of their parents left millions of other children on their own. Many ended up in orphanages—intended for those under the age of six-teen—but others roamed the streets begging or joined the children's gangs.... Some children slipped through the system and were left to fend for them-selves. Mikhail Mironov was ten years old when his parents were arrested in 1936. They were both factory workers from the Ukraine, Red partisans in the Civil War, who had risen through the ranks of the Party ... before their arrests.... So Mikhail was alone. For a while, he lived with various relatives, but he was a burden to them all.... His aunt Bela, who had taken care of Mikhail in the previous months, saw it as an opportunity to be rid of him, and sent him off to live in the student dormitory attached to the House of Pioneers.... His only contact was with his mother, and he wrote to her often in the labor camps of Vorkuta. He was isolated and lonely, without friends or family.... Expelled from the dormitory in the House of Pioneers, he found a room in the barracks. **"It is very boring for me,"** the fifteen-year-old boy wrote to his mother in July. "There is no one here. Everyone has gone, and I am on my own." (pp. 329–330)

Children, like Mikhail, who were left on their own, entered an inherently anomic situation which led to loneliness and boredom. As they were children, without a strong sense of identity, their case is exceptional, and their boredom is best cap-tured by the 'Anglo style' of not knowing yourself and by extension, not knowing how to organize your time.

Some have posited that boredom in the Soviet Union was common. The *Homo Sovieticus* felt bored because his society did not provide the right kind of guidance for determining his identity and for adjusting to its structure. Jerphagnon (1997) as quoted by Narusyte (2010) supports this view:

> when the environment was presented as if it were given a priori, and the subject could not change it; when everything seemed to be preplanned ... when subjective time had lost value everything seemed to be banal and boredom was the dominant state of mind. (p. 130)

Narusyte continues to elaborate:

> The need for more varied information, transcendence or meaning **could only be realized individually and secretly, and this amounted to an act of spiritual independence and resistance** ... as Otto Fenichel

[an Austrian psychoanalyst] termed it: a Soviet citizen could 'justifiably' blame the society and the state for his or her boredom. (p. 131)

Hence, Soviet citizens coped with their horribly meaningless environment of propaganda and state encouraged 'hard work' by retreating into their inner world of passionately developing their interests and persona and privately constructing a strong and unshakeable sense of identity. Narusyte (2010, p. 132) explains: "The individual refuses to participate in a game whose rules are set by ideology, resisting the conformist existence of an alien and aggressive society". As Soviet society was as rigid as citizens' sense of self, attempting to adapt their identity to society often proved useless and disastrous, and sometimes lethal (as in the countless cases for whom 'rebellion' resulted in the penalty of death for themselves and often for their extended families). A high-profile example is the case of the Nobel Prize winning author Aleksandr Solzhenitsyn who was falsely accused of anti-Soviet propaganda and imprisoned in the Gulag internment camp system for being exceptionally and threateningly talented. He survived the camp and was persecuted throughout his life by the USSR.

Some scholarship suggests that long after the revolution and Stalin's Reign, Soviet boredom continued and expressed itself in an interesting youth culture. Referencing, sociologist Paul Willis (1978), Klapp (1986) notes that the Soviet youth of the 1970s were bored and to the shock of their parents, expressed their boredom in avoiding state-led social spaces such as clubs while acting out by drinking and smoking in crowds after school and dressing in Western fashion. Drinking heavily grew to epidemic proportions and became the leading cause of death in the Soviet Union and current day Russia. Soviet youth culture provides an interesting case of using the newfound freedom of smoking, drinking, and wearing Western fashion as a distraction from boredom.

19th and 20th century gendered experiences

In order to more fully understand the experience of boredom, it is important to consider gender distinctions. This section is deliberately placed, towards the end, to allow us to engage with cases presented throughout the book.

Although both men and women experienced chronic bouts of boredom, their experiences diverged. It appears that, as in the case of Stalinist and post-WWII American housewives, disillusionment played a critical role. Being a house wife was their primary identity, and they imagined that they would enjoy marriage and domesticity. However, 'housewife' is a relational role which requires connecting with one's husband and receiving societal recognition for one's contribution.

Table 5.3 Historical cases of boring gender roles

←***Male***—Soviet revolutionaries—Civil servants of 19th century British colonialism and their wives—Stalinist era orphans—Stalinist era housewives/post-WWII suburban American housewives (Friedan)—***Female***→

In both cases, due to their husbands work requirements of often being away and busy, and societal norms, such desires went unmet. However, in many respects, American housewives were better off than their Soviet counterparts because of a better quality of life in the US and a general societal acceptance and respect for their role as important and valuable. Interestingly, Stalinist-era housewives often internally resisted both Communist ideology and Soviet propaganda against them.

Disillusionment also played a primary role in the existential and chronic boredom of Soviet revolutionaries. They felt most alive fighting and struggling for their dream of communist utopia. Once they achieved deposing the Tsar and the creation of the USSR, they were unable to imagine other big goals. Their primary identity was that of a revolutionary and the revolution had ended successfully. They were left muscling through the drudgery of monotonous Soviet life. Their strong patriotism, pride, and stamina for war, had no outlet. These 'gladiators' experienced 'the psychopathology of everyday life', imprisoned in monotonous government jobs and in prisons of domesticity, leading a bland civilian life. To soothe their thwarted desires and tolerate their unbearable dis-ease, many turned to alcohol.

As prior examples demonstrate, the subjective inability to fulfil one's societal gender role played a major role in triggering boredom. Although Friedan's ([1963] 2013) famous study of American housewives emphasized the boredom of women, more recently, peer-reviewed scholarship on boredom has found that men experience more boredom than women (Chin et al. 2016; Farmer & Sundberg, 1986; Mikulas & Vodanovich 1993; Sundberg et al. 1991; Wallace, Vodanovich, & Restino 2003). As studies have shown that educational-attainment negatively correlates with boredom (Mann & Robinson 2009; Robinson 1975; Wegner et al. 2008), it may be the missing link in explaining a possible shift from boredom being predominant in women to its more-recent prominence in male experience. Historically, as women's educational attainment has increased, relative to men, their boredom has declined.

Note

1 Starting with the 1980s, Soviet citizens began comically referring to themselves as a unique species of man—*Homo Sovieticus* (Fitzpatrick 1999).

Conclusion

Modernity's revolutionary challenge

> For too long we have been dreaming a dream from which we are now waking up: the dream that if we just improve the socioeconomic situation of people, everything will be play, people will become happy. The truth is that as the **struggle for survival** has subsided, the question has emerged: **survival for what?** Even more people today have means to live but no meaning to live for.
>
> Viktor Frankl (1978)

As social scientists, we aim to understand and advance the knowledge of humanity. This is a grand task with a high bar of ethics, methodology, and long-term marathon-level stamina. As contemporary sociologists, attempting to peek into even one phenomenon of modernity often seems colossal and unsurmountable. We are poignantly aware of the limits of our knowledge, consciousness, and scientific capacity to honestly capture humanity *as is*. If we are fortunate, we stumble upon a discovery and theory that lends us insight into its greater context.

I arrived at the study of boredom as a sociologist, a practicing psychotherapist, an avid reader of Western literature and philosophy, as a classically-trained portrait painter with an interest in art history, and as a former immigrant from the Soviet Union. As a reader, I noticed that Western literature and philosophy served as a sobbing cry of misery and boredom. Boredom in particular struck me as a perplexing focus amongst elite intellectual writers whose minds were genius, filled with seemingly cosmic revelation into humanity's predicament, who belonged to a community of intellectuals with whom they could converse and connect, and who wrote during a time of revolutionary social and economic progress. I would regularly wonder: Why are the intellectual crème of the crop bored? Doesn't being intellectual assume a rich inner world and preclude boredom? Could boredom have motivated their writing and, more generally, driven the creation of contemporary Western literature? As a portrait painter, with a strong background in art's historical trajectory, I noticed that its Renaissance principles were denounced at around WWI and that even after many years of swimming in the art world, my understanding and personal preference for modern art was weak. While strongly touched by Rembrandt and Michelangelo, and until my discovery of modern art's focus on the *Aesthetic of Indifference*, I continued to be perplexed by the 'novel' and 'trendy' monochromatic canvas.

While as a psychotherapist, I noticed that boredom was common amongst my patients and often pre-dated their decline into clinical depression and anxiety. I found that once their boredom and the subjective meaninglessness of their lives resolved, so did their mental illness. I decided to make boredom my subject of study for three years and the topic of my first book. My cross-cultural life experiences and professional duality allowed me to historically and systematically explore boredom in Anglo and Russian society, as well as within the realm of art.

A cross-cultural comparison would allow insight into the cultural foundation and cultural boundaries of the phenomenon and would personally help me understand my two cultures and languages more deeply. Echoing Frankl (1978) in the quote at the top of this chapter, as a Western civilization, we 'progressed' from dying from starvation to dying from boredom, as the latter experience has come to infect many of our waking hours and drive much of our social ills: violence, crime, war, terrorism, self-harm, and potentially mental illness. This allows us to contemplate and evaluate the actual quality of our social progress as well as the impact of a shift in cultural-economic-temporal conditions.

Methodologically, I chose comparative historical analysis, primary sources such as letters, dictionaries, representative literature, and published studies and statistics for importing and analyzing supporting cases, as these investigation techniques were well-suited to my research and would provide access to historical emergence and variability. Given the private nature, subtlety, variation of expression of the phenomenon of boredom, and its recent historicity, I decided against limiting my research to in-depth interviews, analysis of survey data, and ethnography of those identifying as 'bored' as such methods would not offer access to boredom's historical and sociological emergence. Humanity and the collective, as socio-culturally-historically situated, became my unit of analysis. My primary research questions were: 1. When and why did the neologism and phenomenon of boredom emerge? 2. What were the historical and sociological circumstances that led to the creation of this new word and concept? 3. Is the experience of boredom culturally variable? 4. What are its cultural manifestations? 5. How does it relate to art, politics, and activism? 6. Do sensory underload and overload always lead to boredom? These queries were well-suited for comparative historical methodology and published studies on sensory stimulation and deprivation. Collaterally, I analyzed published letters, survey data, and ethnographic observations, and did not think that designing my own in-depth interview, survey, or ethnography would offer me additional findings or assist in better answering my queries.

More broadly, this study contributes to our knowledge of the sociology of emotion, particularly to the cultural boundaries of emotional experience, as well as to social theory, cultural and cognitive sociology, sociolinguistics, anomie, gender and sexuality, symbolic interactionism, mental health, modernity, art, political sociology, the sociology of everyday experience, and to an emerging literature on the sociology of time, time use, and waiting. My findings engage with the critical debate on cross-cultural experience, the impact of globalization and the spread of *Western emotional experience* and norms such as the prohibition against wasting time, inequalities around waiting, and problematize assumptions around *the timeless nature of emotions*. In line with this, my study responds to academic and popular essentialist portrayals of 'boredom' as having always existed across time and space and is in conversation with the sociology of the everyday which conceptualizes boredom as common and democratic. It is also in conversation with those exploring the *death* of traditional art as well as those interested in the cause of violent political activism, terrorism, and the recent rise of authoritarian leadership.

Throughout this book, I attempt to revive an interest in the study of common 'everyday' experience which was pioneered by sociologists Henri Lefebvre and Guy Debord. I demonstrate that while contemporary art has adopted an *Aesthetic of Indifference* and activism, a stance of 'no opinion', sociology has shown little interest in experiences that are easily and commonly enacted by most, as well as in the institution of art and in humanity's experience of time. My book aims to close this gap and considers experiences of lack and emptiness worthy of study. As in the cases of art and activism adopting 'boredom' and 'no opinion' as a strategy, I aim to show that investigating the boring can be provocative. While in terms of 'time', I hope for this book to serve as a call for inquiry into the temporal structure of experience, historically, institutionally, and cross-culturally. An institution's temporal rhythms may facilitate the emotional spectrum of excitement to boredom. The identification of such rhythms would be useful for social organization, schooling, psychiatry, and industry.

In regard to the modern epidemic of functional mental illness, boredom is a common symptom of depression known as anhedonia and is defined as an inability to feel pleasure. As a practicing psychotherapist, I have observed that a phase of anhedonia often preexists the onset of major depression and schizophrenia. For weeks or months, patients will complain of feeling painful boredom with their life circumstances, with eating, socializing, jobs, and family, and with life in general. If their boredom fails to resolve, they often fall into a deep clinical depression, and begin depending on psychotropic medicine to combat their painful experience. Further investigation will establish whether more aggressively diagnosing anhedonia could flag those at risk for developing functional mental illness and be used as a prevention tool.

Although boredom has become synonymous with modernity's zeitgeist, it is culturally-bound and expresses itself differently depending on the context. As simple boredom cannot be sustained indefinitely, eventually it progresses to the existential variety in which existence itself becomes burdensome. Anglo boredom is an extension of the 'you can be whatever you want to be' culture and is symptomatic of an identity crisis resulting from surplus options than is possible to process and integrate, leading to paralysis. Hit with Anglo boredom, one finds oneself either desperately attempting to distract from the experience (as in treading water), upholding it as a status symbol, or resigning to flouting in nonaction. While Russian boredom is an extension of 'I have a solid identity that society ignores or disregards'. While the Anglo problematic is resolvable with healthy identity formation and commitment, the Russian problematic generally remains irresolvable, often leading to suicide. The latter can only be transmuted with a restructuring of society and a gross advancement of opportunities. In the current political climate of dictatorship, poor human rights and poor economy, societal improvement remains a moot point as do opportunities for those chronically-bored.

This study also makes claims relevant to sociolinguistics. Although in English, boredom connotes idleness and a neutral valence, in Russian, boredom is more intensely charged. In English, boredom and anguish are semantic opposites, while in Russian they are adjacent. For example, Dostoyevsky's *The Brothers Karamazov* ([1879–1880] 2002) describes a horrific style of boredom orchestrated by the devil who literally can bore one to death. In Russian, boredom is often conceptualized as founded on emptiness and terror. This extends to institutionalized boredom deliberately implemented for the purposes of social control, as in case of Stalin's dinner parties and in the Soviet case of regularly and indefinitely waiting in line for rations of food and clothes, while aware that rations would likely run out and that your family would remain hungry and cold. Having one's citizens spend their limited unorganized time waiting in line may have offered a convenient form of social control.

Importantly, my findings suggest that although a changing sensory environment is critical for healthy mental and emotional functioning, meaning-making and timespan remain more important in determining subjective experience. Hence, some do find meaning and make good use of both solitary confinement and sensory deprivation. Solitary confinement is especially interesting as it results in 'social death' of identity to the outside world and as it deliberately uses boredom as a method of punishment. Research suggests that some inmates appreciate their confinement and use it productively as a container for intellectual pursuit, such as writing books and litigation (John Doe as referenced by Suedfeld et al. 1982 p. 308; Gaddis 1957). Some people may not require intense external stimulation as they have a rich internal world and passionate interests for self-pursuit, or they are able to transmute a necessity into a virtue and utilize their solitude productively.

Suedfeld et al. (1990 p. xiii) found that time-limited sensory deprivation, especially in a floating tank, led to psychological and physiological deep relaxation and was described by subjects as "enjoyable" and "extremely pleasant" and increased their cognitive and behavioral capacity. Studies have shown that solitary confinement can even prove therapeutic in niche cases. Van Putten (1973) and Harris (1959) found that schizophrenic patients who were non-responsive to active inpatient treatment improved when exposed to solitary confinement; their hallucinations and psychosis decreased or stopped and they reported finding life more tolerable. Smith et al. (1961) suggests that isolation is the most comfortable environment for those with schizophrenia as it decreases the number and intensity of disturbing internal events. Boredom can be self-perpetuating. The bored individual struggles with sluggish mental capacity and will, inviting a continuation of boredom. External sensory underload or overload leads to a deadening of internal activity. However, one's threshold for an ideal level or the 'sweet spot' of sensory stimulation is variable depending on factors such as self-directive ability and desire to engage in a solitary creative project, stress-level, and psychiatric dis-ease.

My study places boredom as a central experience of modern society of the 21st century through popular idioms (ex. *the daily grind* and *hump day*) and statistics which establish boredom as common. Attack on rest, sleep, and wasting time, medicating and technologically-distracting 'overactive' children and adults, as well as the societal encouragement of hourly productivity are symptomatic of this phenomenon. It explores the schism between traditional art which is imbued with meaning, entertainment-value, and offers powerful distraction with the modern *Aesthetic of Indifference* which deliberately produces redundancy, chaos, silence, and nothingness. Additionally, it explores the role of exposure to surplus information in simulating anomie and driving boredom. I consider boredom as a protective spam filter to sort and block unhelpful information while saving mental energy.

Although this book serves as a social critique of modernity, I would like to emphasize the historically revolutionary and empowering qualities of individualism and self-drive, and the impossibility of dialing the clocks to premodernity. Underlining the hypocrisy of modern social critics on their unrealistic and fantastical desire for *others* to return to a prior historical period, deny themselves the fruits of modernity, force social cohesion, as well as on their 'functionalist' tendencies, Riesman ([1950] 2001) writes:

> Many critics of contemporary life would move … on the assumption that people have not too little freedom but too much. Some of these critics speak from a religious platform, others out of a preoccupation with urban anomie. … Rather, they would like to freeze people into communities in which friendship will be based largely on propinquity. They are apt to share the outlook of the city planner who said that he thought the ideal communities in America were to be found among the rural … of the deep South and the French Canadians of the Quebec villages…. Here we find the classes attempting to force "roots" upon the masses…. We might term those critics the neotraditionalists. They seem to want to deny to others the privileges of modern society which, however, they themselves take as a matter of course. Their own choice is for French food one day and Italian the next; they select their ideas from all ages and their friends from all places; they enjoy primitive African and Renaissance Italian sculpture and read books in four languages. These are felt as advantages, not liabilities; and it is ironic that many sophisticated other-directed people, out of fear, impatience, fashion, and boredom, express nostalgia for a time in the past in which they could not have had such choices. (p. 278)

In line with Riesman's sentiment, there is a hypocrisy to romanticizing the lost past while enjoying the fruits of the present. Since modernity, the world is forever altered. One might even say that anomie-saturated modernity serves as an emergent phenomenon. We cannot and would not privilege returning to a rigidly stratified and scripted society. As Todd Gitlin writes in the forward to *The Lonely Crowd* ([1950] 2001 p. xxv): "There is also in our high and popular culture preference for anomie over adjustment", and the latter includes tradition, role stratification, conformism, and more generally unfreedom. In terms of its consequences, modernity has offered us a quid pro quo—countless benefits for the price of stability, predictability, and sanity. This book serves as a challenge to sociologists and the public to transmute anomie into a life that's radically in one's one image and to create institutions that promote self-knowing and self-thriving, with appropriate support for the struggling.

This scholarship is as an example of fruition from developing classic sociological theory. I have always been impressed by the explanatory power of Durkheim's anomie, yet realized that there were critical complementary factors. My work identifies two complimentary explanatory factors: temporality and present-focus, rarely explored by Sociology. I show that boredom requires present-focused, is driven by anomie, and is amplified by extended time, allowing me to articulate a more accurate story of boredom.

As we all experience boredom, this study advances the analysis of the everyday of modern society of the 20th and 21st centuries and aims to expose the unremarkable as remarkable. This scholarship is inherently democratic and important as it aims to understand an experience common to most and to tell 'our story', which is too often overlooked and taken-for-granted. I wholeheartedly believe that boredom is 'the' modern problematic and the most crucial issue of our generation.

References

Afanas'ev, Aleksandr N. 1916. "The Princess Who Would Not Smile", pp. 133–137 in *Russian Folk-Tales*. New York: E. P. Dutton & Company.

American Psychological Association. 2012. "Psychologist Testifies on the Risks of Solitary Confinement". Retrieved July 1, 2019 from www.apa.org/monitor/2012/10/solitary

Amis, Martin. 2009. *The Second Plane: September 11: Terror and Boredom*. USA: Vintage International.

Amos, Amanda, Susie Wiltshire, Sally Haw, & Ann McNeill. 2006. "Ambivalence and Uncertainty: Experiences of and Attitudes Toward Addiction and Smoking Cessation in the Mid-to-Late Teens". *Health Education Research* 21: 181–191. https://doi.org/10.1093/her/cyh054.

Anshel, Mark H. 1991. "Cognitive-Behavioral Strategies for Combating Drug Abuse in Sport: Implications for Coaches and Sport Psychology Consultants". *The Sport Psychologist* 2: 152–166. https://doi.org/10.1123/tsp.5.2.152

Aratani, Lauren. 2019. "Trump Couldn't be Prosecuted if he Shot Someone on Fifth Avenue, Lawyer Claims". *The Guardian*, October 23. Retrieved November 20, 2019 from www.theguardian.com/us-news/2019/oct/23/donald-trump-immune-shoot-fifth-avenue-murder

Arendt, Hannah. 2006. *Eichmann in Jerusalem: A Report on the Banality of Evil*. London: Amos Elan.

Aries, Philippe. 1962. *Centuries of Childhood: A Social History of Family Life*. New York: Vintage Books.

Atran, Scott. 2010. *Talking to the Enemy: Religion, Brotherhood, and the (Un)Making of Terrorists*. New York: Ecco.

Au, Susan. 1988. *Ballet and Modern Dance*. New York: Thames & Hudson.

Barzun, Jacques. 2000. *From Dawn to Decadence: 1500 Years of Western Cultural Life*. New York: HarperCollins Publishers.

Bearden, Lisa J., William A. Spencer, & John C. Moracco. 1989. "A Study of High School Dropouts". *The School Counselor* 2: 113–120.

Belleza, Silvia, Neeru Paharai, & Anat Keinan. 2016. "Conspicuous Consumption of Time: When Busyness and Lack of Leisure Time Become a Status Symbol". *Journal of Consumer Research* 44(1): 118–138. https://doi.org/10.1093/jcr/ucw076

Bellow, Saul. 2008. *Humboldt's Gift*. London: Penguin Classics.

Belton, Teresa. 2016. "Want to be a Great Parent? Let Your Children be Bored". World Economic Forum, September 26. Retrieved August 22, 2018 from www.weforum.org/agenda/2016/09/being-bored-is-good-for-children-and-adults-this-is-why?utm_content=bufferb8f6b&utm_medium=social, & utm_source=twitter.com&utm_campaign=buffer

Bench, Shane W. & Heather C. Lench. 2013. "On the Function of Boredom". *Behavioral Science* 3: 459–472. https://doi.org/10.3390/bs3030459

Benjamin, Walter. 2002. *The Arcades Project*. Cambridge, MA: Belknap Press of Harvard University Press.

Bennetts, Marc. 2018. "Super Putin: Do Russians Really Love Their President?" *Newsweek*, February 12. Retrieved June 4, 2019 from www.newsweek.com/2018/02/16/russians-love-putin-800256.html

Berlyne, D. E. 1960. *Conflict, Arousal, and Curiosity*. New York: McGraw-Hill. http://dx.doi.org/10.1037/11164-000

Berman, Paul. 2004. *Terror and Liberalism*. New York: W. W. Norton, & Company.

Boden, Joseph. 2009. "The Devil Inside: Boredom Proneness and Impulsive Behavior", pp. 203–226 in *Essays on Boredom and Modernity*, edited by Barbara Dalle Pezza and Carlo Salzani. New York: Rodopi.

Bokhari, Allum. 2018. "Leaked Video: Google Leadership's Dismayed Reaction to Trump Election". *Breitbart News Network*, September 12. Retrieved June 3, 2019 from www.breitbart.com/tech/2018/09/12/leaked-video-google-leaderships-dismayed-reaction-to-trump-election/

Bresnahan, Ali. 2017. "Dancing in Time", pp. 339–348 in *The Routledge Handbook of Philosophy and Temporal Experience*, edited by Ian Phillips. New York: Routledge. https://doi.org/10.4324/9781315269641

Britton, Annie, & Martin J. Shipley. 2010. "Bored to Death?". *International Journal of Epidemiology* 39(2): 370–371. https://doi.org/10.1093/ije/dyp404

Brodsky, Joseph. 1995. *On Grief and Reason*. USA: Farrar, Straus & Giroux.

Burton, Robert A. 2017. *The Anatomy of Melancholy*. London: CreateSpace Independent Publishing Platform.

Byron, Lord. 2009. *Childe Harold's Pilgrimage*. Location Unknown: The Floating Press.

Byron, Lord. 2016. *Don Juan*. Great Britain: Pantianos Classics.

Cage, John. 1973. *M: Writings '67–'72*. New York: Wesleyan University Press.

Cage, John. 1961. *Silence*. Middletown, CT: Wesleyan University Press.

Calcagno, Antonio. 2017. "The Life That is not Purely One's Own: Michel Henry and Boredom as an Affect", pp. 53–63 in *Boredom Studies Reader: Frameworks and Perspectives*, edited by Michael E. Gardiner, & Julian J. Haladyn. Abingdon: Routledge. https://doi.org/10.4324/9781315682587

Callimachi, Rukmini. 2015. "Isis and the Lonely Young American". *The New York Times*, June 27. Retrieved January 2, 2020 from www.nytimes.com/2015/06/28/world/americas/isis-online-recruiting-american.html

Cambridge Academic Content Dictionary. 2019. "Bored". Cambridge University Press. Retrieved July 1, 2019 from https://dictionary.cambridge.org/us/dictionary/english/bored

Chances, Ellen B. 1978. *Conformity's Children: An Approach to the Superfluous Man in Russian Literature*. Bloomington, IN: Slavica Publishers.

Chekhov, Anton P. 2011. *Delphi Complete Works of Anton Chekhov*. USA: Delphi Classics.

Chekhov, Anton P. 2019. "Lights". The Literature Network. Retrieved January 5, 2019 from www.online-.literature.com/anton_chekhov/1250/

Chekhov, Anton P. 2016. *The Lady with the Dog: And Other Stories*. USA: Open Road Media.

Cheng, Joyce S. 2007. "Paris Dada and the Transfiguration of Boredom". *Modernism/Modernity* 24(3): 599–628. https://doi.org/10.1353/mod.2017.0051

Chin, Alycia, Amanda Markey, Saurabh Bhargava, Karim S. Kassam, & George Loewenstein. 2016. "Bored in the USA: Experience Sampling and Boredom in Everyday Life". *Emotion* 2: 359–368. http://dx.doi.org/10.1037/emo0000232

Coleridge, Samuel T. 2017. *Lyrical Ballads*. Miami, FL: HardPress.

Cracraft, James. 2004. *The Revolution of Peter the Great*. USA: Harvard University Press.

Csikszentmihalyi, Mihaly. 1990. *Flow: The Psychology of Optimal Experience*. New York: Harper Perennial Modern Classics.

Csikszentmihalyi, Mihaly. 2000. "Happiness, Flow, and Economic Equality". *American Psychologist* 55(10): 1163–1164. https://doi.org/10.1037/0003-066X.55.10.1163

Cummings, Mary L., Fei Gao, & Kris Thornburg. 2016. "Boredom in the Workplace: A New Look at an Old Problem". *Human Factors* 58(2): 279–300. https://doi.org/10.1177/0018720815609503

Davies, Jim, & Mark Fortney. 2012. "The Menton Theory of Engagement and Boredom", pp. 131–143 in *Proceedings of the First Annual Conference on the Advances of Cognitive Systems*, edited P. Langley.

DDI. 2004. "Faking It". *DDI Research Report Autumn 2004*. UK: Development Dimensions International, Inc.

Debord, Guy. 1961. "Perspectives for Conscious Changes in Everyday Life". *Situationist International Online*, May 17. Retrieved June 3, 2019 from www.cddc.vt.edu/sionline/si/everyday.html

de Chenne, Timothy K. 1988. "Boredom as a Clinical Issue". *Psychotherapy* 25: 71–81. https://doi.org/10.1037/h0085325

de Tocqueville, Alexis. 2002. *Democracy in America*. Chicago, IL: University of Chicago Press.

Deutsch, Karl W. 1961. "Social Mobilization and Political Development". *American Political Science Review* 55 (September): 634–647. https://doi.org/10.2307/1952679

Di Giannantonio, Massimo, & Giovanni Martinotti. 2012. "Anhedonia and Major Depression: The Role of Agomelatine". *European Neuropsychopharmacology*, 22 (Suppl 3): S505–S510. https://doi.org/10.1016/j.euroneuro.2012.07.004

Dickens, Charles. 2003. *Bleak House*. London: Wordsworth Classics.

Disraeli. Benjamin. 2017. *Consingsby or the New Generation*. The Project Gutenberg.

Dobrenko, Evgeny, & Eric Naiman. 2011. *The Landscape of Stalinism: The Art and Ideology of Soviet Space*. USA: University of Washington Press.

Donaldson, Tammy M. 2018. "Is Boredom Driving Pigs Crazy?" *Behave: Stories of Applied Animal Behavior*. Retrieved August 22, 2019 from www.webpages.uidaho.edu/range556/Appl_BEHAVE/projects/pigs_ster.html

Dostoyevsky, Fyodor. 2008. *Demons*. London: Penguin Classics.

Dostoyevsky, Fyodor, & Constance Garnett. 1918. *Notes from the Underground*. New York: The MacMillan Company.

Dostoyevsky, Fyodor. 2002. *The Brothers Karamazov*. New York: First Farrar, Straus, & Giroux.

Durkheim, Emile. 1979. *Suicide: A Study in Sociology*. New York: The Free Press.

Durkheim, Emile. 1982. *The Rules of Sociological Method*. New York: Free Press.

Durkheim, Emile, & Lewis A. Coser. 2014. *The Division of Labor in Society*. New York: Free Press.

Eastwood, John D., Alexandra Frischen, Mark J. Fenske, & Daniel Smilek. 2012. "The Unengaged Mind: Defining Boredom in Terms of Attention". *Sage Journals* 5: 482–495. https://doi.org/10.1177/1745691612456044

Eliot, George. 1996. *Daniel Deronda*. London: Penguin Group.

Effimova, Alla. 1994. "Photographic Ethics in the Work of Boris Mikhailov", pp. 181–183 in *Boredom*, edited by Tom McDonough. Cambridge, MA: The MIT Press.

Ekman, Paul. 1984. "Expression and the Nature of Emotion", pp. 319–344 in *Approaches to Emotion*, edited by Klaus R. Scherer, & Paul Ekman, Hillsdale, NJ: Lawrence Erlbaum.

Eligon, John. 2016. "Bored, Broke and Armed: Clues to Chicago's Gang Violence". *The New York Times*, December 22. Retrieved August 22, 2017 from www.nytimes.com/2016/12/22/us/chicago-gang-violence.html?mcubz=1

Estrada-Salazer, Christopher. 2019. "Opinion: Art is Dead, and We Killed It". *The Student Life*, April 10. Retrieved December 20, 2019 from https://tsl.news/opinion-art-is-dead/

Familyconnect.org. 2019. "Repetitive Behaviors in Blind Children: What Are They?" FamilyConnect: For Parents of Children with Visual Impairments. Retrieved June 3, 2019 from www.familyconnect.org/info/browse-by-age/infants-and-toddlers/social-life-and-recreation-iandt/repetitive-behaviors/1235

Farmer, Richard, & Norman D. Sundberg 1986. "Boredom Proneness—The Development and Correlates of a New Scale". *Journal of Personality Assessment*, 50: 4–17. https://doi.org/10.1207/s15327752jpa5001_2

Ferrell, Jeff. 2004. "Boredom, Crime and Criminology". *Theoretical Criminology* 8(3): 287–302. https://doi.org/10.1177/1362480604044610

Figes, Orlando. 2008. *The Whisperers: Private Life in Stalin's Russia*. New York: Orlando Figes.

Fisher, Cynthia D. 1987. "Boredom: Construct, Causes and Consequences". *Human Resources Research* February: 1–36.

Fisher, Cynthia D. 1993. "Boredom at Work: A Neglected Concept". *Sage Journals* 3: 395–417. https://doi.org/10.1177/001872679304600305

Fitzpatrick, Sheila. 1999. *Everyday Stalinism: Ordinary Life in Extraordinary Times: Soviet Russia in the 1930s*. New York: Oxford University Press, Inc.

Fording, Richard C., & Stanford F. Schram. 2017. "The Cognitive and Emotional Sources of Trump Support: The Case of Low-Information Voters". *New Political Science* 39(4): 670–686. https://doi.org/10.1080/07393148.2017.1378295

Frankl, Viktor E. 1975. *The Unconscious God: Psychotherapy and Theology*. New York: Simon & Schuster.

Frankl, Viktor E. 1978. *The Unheard Cry for Meaning*. New York: Simon & Schuster.

Frankl, Viktor E. 1986. *The Doctor and the Soul: From Psychotherapy to Logotherapy*. New York: Vintage Books.

Frey, Carl B., Thor Berger, & Chinchih Chen. 2017. "Political Machinery: Automation Anxiety and the 2016 U.S. Presidential Election". www.oxfordmartin.ox.ac.uk/downloads/academic/Political%20Machinery-Automation%20Anxiety%20and%20the%202016%20U_S_%20Presidential%20Election_230712.pdf

Frey, Carl B., Thor Berger, & Chinchih Chen. 2018. "Political machinery: Did Robots Swing the 2016 US Presidential Election?" *Oxford Review of Economic Policy* 34(3): 418–442. https://doi.org/10.1093/oxrep/gry007

Friedan, Betty. 2013. *The Feminine Mystique*. New York: W.W. Norton, & Company.

Friedman, Richard A. 2014. "A Natural Fix for A.D.H.D.". *The New York Times*, October 31. Retrieved August 22, 2017 from www.nytimes.com/2014/11/02/opinion/sunday/a-natural-fix-for-adhd.html

Frost, Natasha. 2018. "For 11 Years, the Soviet Union Had No Weekends". *A&E Television Networks*, August 30. Retrieved April 11, 2019 from www.history.com/news/soviet-union-stalin-weekend-labor-policy

Gaddis, Thomas E. 1957. *Birdman of Alcatraz*. London: Gollancz.

Gallup. 2016. "Congress and the Public". Retrieved December 20, 2019 from https://news.gallup.com/poll/1600/congress-public.aspx

Galton, Francis G. 1885. "The Measure of Fidget". *Nature* 32: 174–175.

Garber, Megan. 2020. "Boredom is Winning". *The Atlantic*, February 5. Retrieved February 6, 2020 from www.theatlantic.com/culture/archive/2020/02/trump-weinstein-and-politics-boredom/606130/

Gardiner, Michael E., & Julian J. Haladyn. 2017. *Boredom Studies Reader: Frameworks. and Perspectives*. Abingdon: Routledge. https://doi.org/10.4324/9781315682587

Garnett, Constance, & Anton Chekhov. 2014. *My Life: The Story of a Provincial*. USA: CreateSpace Independent Publishing Platform.

Gaviria, Marcela. 2001. "Medicating Kids". Frontline. Retrieved May 15, 2019 from www.pbs.org/wgbh/pages/frontline/shows/medicating/etc/credits.html

Gasparov, Boris. 2008. *Five Operas and a Symphony: Word and Music in Russian Culture*. New Haven: Yale University Press.

Genzlinger, Neil. 2018. "Oskar Rabin, Defiant Artist During Soviet Era, Dies at 90". *The New York Times*, November 11. Retrieved January 25, 2019 from www.nytimes.com/2018/11/11/obituaries/oskar-rabin-defiant-artist-during-soviet-era-dies-at-90.html

Goetz, Thomas, & Anne C. Frenzel. 2006. "Phanomenologie Schulischer Langeweile [Phenomenology of Boredom at School]". *Zeitschrift fur Entwicklungspycheologie und Padogogische Psychologie* 4: 149–153. https://dx.doi.org/10.1026/0049-8637.38.4.149

Goetz, Thomas, Nathan C. Hall, Ulrike E. Nett, Reinhard Pekrun, & Anastasiya A. Lipnevich. 2013. "Types of Boredom: An Experience Sampling Approach". *Motivation and Emotion* 3: 401–419. https://dx.doi.org/10.1007/s11031-013-9385-y

Goffman, Erving. 2017. *Interaction Ritual: Essays in Face-to-Face Behavior*. Abingdon: Routledge. https://doi.org/10.4324/9780203788387

Gogol, Nicolai V. 2003. *Dead Souls*. Mineola, New York:Dover Publications, Inc.

Gogol, Nicolai V., & Leonard J. Kent. 1985. *The Complete Tales of Nikolai Gogol* (Volume 1). USA: Cambridge University Press.

Goncharov, Ivan A. 2005. *Oblomov*. Harmondsworth, UK: Penguin.

Gooding, Judson. 1976. "How to Cope with Boredom". *Reader's Digest* 108(51): 51–57.

Goodstein, Elizabeth S. 2005. *Experience Without Qualities: Boredom and Modernity*. Stamford, CA: Stamford University Press.

Google Trends. 2019. *Google Public Data*.

Gore, Catherine. 2017. *Romances of Real Life*. Miami, FL: HardPress.

Gosline, Anne. 2007. "Bored to Death: Chronically Bored People Exhibit Higher Risk-Taking Behavior". *Scientific American*, February 26. Retrieved August 22, 2017 from www.scientificamerican.com/article/the-science-of-boredom/

Gouda, Moaman, & Markus Marktanner. 2018. "Muslim Youth Unemployment and Expat Jihadism: Bored to Death?". *Studies in Conflict, & Terrorism* 42(10): 878–897. https://doi.org/10.1080/1057610X.2018.1431316

Grant, Bruce. 2009. *The Captive and the Gift: Cultural Histories of Sovereignty in Russia and the Caucasus*. Ithaca, New York:Cornell University Press.

Green, Peter. 2014. *Final Exam: A Novel*. London: PublishNation.

Green, Stephen. 2019. "The Thrill Is Gone? Dems Seem Bored with Their Presidential Candidates". PJ Media, August 21. Retrieved October 19, 2019 from https://pjmedia.com/vodkapundit/the-thrill-is-gone-dems-seem-bored-with-their-presidential-candidates/

Grove, Thomas. 2018. "Czar Vladimir? Putin Acolytes Want to Bring Back the Monarchy". *The Wall Street Journal*, December 13. Retrieved January 11 2019 from www.wsj.com/articles/czar-vladimir-putin-acolytes-want-to-bring-back-the-monarchy-11544732680

Guyau, Jean-Marie. 2017. *The Non-Religion of the Future*. USA: CreateSpace Independent Publishing Platform.

Haladyn, Julian J. 2011. "Empire of the Boring: The Unbearable Duration of Andy Warhol's Films". *Kinema: A Journal of Film and Audiovisual Media* 34: 105–113.

Haladyn, Julian J. 2015. *Boredom and Art: Passions of the Will to Boredom*. Winchester, UK: Zero Books.

Haque, Omar S., Jihye Choi, Time Phillips, & Harold Bursztajn. 2015. "Why are Young Westerners Drawn to Terrorist Organizations like ISIS?" *Psychiatric Times* 32(9).

Harden, Blaine. 1982. "BORING! BORING! Boring! Boring! Boring!" *The Washington Post Magazine*, January 31. Retrieved January 20, 2019 from www.washingtonpost.com/archive/opinions/1982/01/31/boring-boring-boring-boring-boring/d3350f34-19d4-4f99-a04f-7bd8148928d6/

Harju, Lotta K., & Jarri J. Hakanen. 2016. "An Employee who was Not There: A Study of Job Boredom in White-Collar Work". *Personnel Review, Farnborough* 45(2): 374–391. https://doi.org/10.1108/PR-05-2015-0125

Harris, A. 1959. "Sensory Deprivation and Schizophrenia". *Journal of Mental Sciences* 105: 235–237. https://doi.org/10.1192/bjp.105.438.235

Haydon, Benjamin R. 1831. *Waiting for the Times*. London: The Bridgeman Art Library.

Healy, Sean D. 1984. *Boredom, Self, and Culture*. US: Fairleigh Dickinson University Press.

Hennely, Robert. 2019. "Labor Leaders Fear the DNC is Alienating Voters with Boring Debates". Salon, November 24. Retrieved December 15, 2019 from www.salon.com/2019/11/24/labor-leaders-fear-the-dnc-is-alienating-voters-with-boring-debates/

Henry, Michel. 2013. *Barbarism*. London: Continuum International Publishing Group.

Higgins, Dick. 1968. "Boredom and Danger", pp. 81–84 in *Boredom*, edited by Tom McDonough, Cambridge, MA: The MIT Press.

Hitesh, Mansi. 2013. *Toska: Love.Life.Loss.* India: Partridge Publishing.

Hoffman, Bruce. 2017. *Inside Terrorism*. New York: Columbia University Press.

Howard, Michael. 2000. *Invention of Peace*. USA: Yale University Press.

IMDB. 2019. "Emak-Bakia". Retrieved January 20, 2019 from www.imdb.com/title/tt0125073/

IMDB. 2019. "The Starfish". Retrieved January 20, 2019 from www.imdb.com/title/tt0146367/

Jacobs, Tom. 2018. "A Cult Expert Finds Familiar Patterns of Behavior in Trump's GOP". *Pacific Standard*, June 21. Retrieved May 20, 2019 from https://psmag.com/news/a-sociologist-explains-the-similarities-between-cults-and-trumps-gop

Jaynes, Julian. 1976. *The Origin of Consciousness in the Break Down of the Bicameral Mind*. USA: First Mariner Books.

Johnsen, Rasmus. 2016. "Boredom and Organization Studies". *Sage Journals* 37: 1403–1415. https://doi.org/10.1177/0170840616640849

Kania, Andrew. 2017. "Music and Time", pp. 349–360 in *The Routledge Handbook of Philosophy and Temporal Experience*, edited by Ian Phillips. New York: Routledge. https://doi.org/10.4324/9781315269641

Kabakov, Ilya. 1992. *The Life of Flies*. Fine Art Biblio. Retrieved June 4, 2019 from https://fineartbiblio.com/artworks/ilya-and-emilia-kabakov/840/the-life-of-flies

Kahn, Nathaniel. 2018. *The Price of Everything*. HBO Films.

Kandinsky, Wassily. 1977. *Concerning the Spiritual in Art*. USA: Dover Publications, Inc.

Kempton, Sally. 2014. *Doorways to the Infinite: The Art and Practice of Tantric Meditation*. Sounds True.

Khan, Shamus R. 2011. *Privilege: The Making of an Adolescent Elite at St. Paul's School*. Princeton, NJ: Princeton University Press.

Kierkegaard, Soren. 2009. *Repetition and Philosophical Crumbs*. Oxford: Oxford University Press.

Kireevskii, Vasilevich, Boris Jakim, & Aleksey Khomiakov. 1998. *On Spiritual Unity: A Slavophile Reader*. Hudson, New York: Lindisfarne Books.

Klapp, Orrin E. 1986. *Overload and Boredom: Essays on the Quality of Life in the Information Society*. Westport, Connecticut: Greenwood Press, Inc.

Krasko, Genrich L. 2004. *The Unbearable Boredom of Being: A Crisis of Meaning in America*. USA: iUniverse, Inc.

Kureishi, Hanif. 1990. *The Buddha of Suburbia*. New York: Penguin Books.

Kurzban, Robert, Angela Duckworth, Joseph W. Kable, & Justus Myers. 2013. "An Opportunity Cost Model of Subjective Effort and Task Performance". *Behavioral and Brain Sciences* 36: 661–679. http://10.1017/S0140525X12003196

Kustermans, Jorg, & Erik Ringmar. 2011. "Modernity, Boredom and War: A Suggestive Essay". *Review of International Political Economy* 37(4): 1775–1792. https://doi.org/10.1017/S0260210510001038

Laugesen, Amanda. 2012. *"Boredom is the Enemy": The Intellectual and Imaginative Lives of Australian Soldiers in the Great War and Beyond*. New York: Ashgate Publishing.

Liddiard, Patrick. 2019. "Is Populism Really a Problem for Democracy?" *HAPP*. Occasional Papers 1–29.

Lermontov, Mikhail. 2002. *A Hero of Our Time*. Woodstock, & New York: Ardis Publishers.

Levinson, Jerrold. 1990. "The Concept of Music", pp. 267–278 in *Music, Art, and Metaphysics*, edited by Jerrold Levinson. Ithaca, New York:Cornell University Press.

Lin, Tan. 2001. "Warhol's Aura and the Language of Writing". *Cabinetmagazine.org*. Retrieved May 22, 2019 from www.cabinetmagazine.org/issues/4/lin.php

Linder, Staffan B. 1970. *The Harried Leisure Class*. USA: Columbia University Press.

Linton, Ralph. 1936. *The Study of Man*. NY: Appleton-Century.

Madison, Greg A. 2009. *The End of Belonging: Untold Stories of Leaving Home and the Psychology of Global Relocation*. Scotts Valley, CA: CreateSpace Independent Publishing Platform.

Magritte, René. 2019. "The Treachery of Images". Retrieved September 4, 2019 from www.renemagritte.org/the-treachery-of-images.jsp

Maeland, Bård, & Paul O. Brunstad. 2009. *Enduring Military Boredom: From 1750 to the Present*. UK: Palgrave Macmillan. https://doi.org/10.1057/9780230244719

Mann, Sandi. 2007. "The Boredom Boom". *The Psychologist* 20(2), 90–93.

Mann, Sandi. 2016. *The Upside of Downtime: Why Boredom is Good*. Great Britain: Robinson.

Mann, Sandi, & Andrew Robinson. 2009. "Boredom in the Lecture Theatre: An Investigation into the Contributors, Moderators and Outcomes of Boredom Amongst University Students". *British Educational Research Journal* 35: 243–258. https://doi.org/10.1080/01411920802042911

Markham, Laura. 2019. "Handling Boredom: Why It's Good for Your Child". *Aha!. Parenting*. Retrieved June 3, 2019 from www.ahaparenting.com/parenting-tools/intelligent-creative-child/boredom-busters-good-for-kids

Martincic, Julia. 2016. "Let It Bleed—Art's Revival of Menstrual Blood". *The Guardian*. Retrieved September 4, 2019 from www.theguardian.com/lifeandstyle/2016/dec/12/let-it-bleed-arts-revival-of-menstrual-blood

McDonough, Tom. 2017. *Boredom*. Cambridge, MA: The MIT Press.

Mead, Margaret, Geoffrey Gorer, & John Rickman. 2001. *Russian Culture*. New York: Berghahn Books.

Meier, Richard L. 1962. *A Communications Theory of Urban Growth*. Cambridge, MA: The MIT Press.

Mercer-Lynn, Kimberley B., David B. Flora, Shelley A. Fahlman, & John D. Eastwood. 2013. "The Measurement of Boredom: Differences Between Existing Self-Report Scales". *Sage Journals* 5: 585–596. https://doi.org/10.1177/1073191111408229

Mestrovic, Stjepan G. 1993. *Emile Durkheim and the Reformation of Sociology*. Lanham, MD: Rowman & Littlefield Publishers, Inc.

Mikulas, William L., & Stephen J. Vodanovich. 1993. "The Essence of Boredom". *The Psychological Record*, 43(1): 3–12.

Miller, James G. 1960. "Information Input Overload and Psychopathology". *The American Journal of Psychiatry* 116(8): 695–704. https://doi.org/10.1176/ajp.116.8.695

Moon, David. 2001. *The Abolition of Serfdom in Russia 1762–1907*. Harlow & London: Longman.

Moran, Joe. 2003. "Benjamin and Boredom". *Critical Quarterly* 45(1–2): 168–181. https://doi.org/10.1111/1467-8705.00483

Morrissey, Siobhan. 2019. "What's This Banana Art Masterpiece Worth? If You Have To Ask…" *Miami Herald*, December 4. Retrieved December 28, 2019 from www.miamiherald.com/entertainment/visual-arts/art-basel/article238038389.html

Morrissey, Susan K. 2007. *Suicide and the Body Politic in Imperial Russia*. Cambridge, UK: Cambridge University Press. https://doi.org/10.1017/CBO9780511496806

Narusyte, Agne. 2010. *The Aesthetics of Boredom: Lithuanian Photography 1980–1990*. Vilnius: Vilniaus Dailes Akademija.

Newberry, Angela L., & Renae D. Duncan. 2001. "Roles of Boredom and Life Goals in Juvenile Delinquency". *Journal of Applied Social Psychology* 3: 527–541. https://doi.org/10.1111/j.1559-1816.2001.tb02054.x

O'Bannon, Isaac M. 2017. "Workplace Boredom Kills Productivity". *CPA Practice Advisor* 27(10): 18.

O'Brien, Wendell. 2014. "Boredom". *Analysis* 74: 236–244. https://doi.org/10.1093/analys/anu041

O'Hanlon, James F. 1981. "Boredom: Practical Consequences and a Theory". *Acta Psychologica* 1: 53–82. https://doi.org/10.1016/0001-6918(81)90033-0

Online Etymology Dictionary. 2019. "Bore". Retrieved June 3, 2019 from www.etymonline.com/index.php?term=bore

Orchardson, William Q. 1883. *The Marriage of Convenience*. Glasgow: Museum Kelvingrove Glasgow Scotland Culture and Sport Glasgow Museums.

Orleck, Annelise. 1999. *The Soviet Jewish Americans*. Westport, CT: Greenwood Press.

Ortega y Gasset, J. 2019. *The Dehumanization of Art and Other Essays on Art, Culture, and. Literature*. Princeton, NJ: Princeton University Press.

Orwell, George. 2018. *Burmese Days: A Novel*. New York: Houghton Mifflin Publishing Company.

Oxford Dictionaries. 2019. "Bored". Retrieved August 22, 2018 from https://en.oxforddictionaries.com/definition/us/bored

Paperno, Irina. 1997. *Suicide as a Cultural Institution in Dostoyevsky's Russia*. Ithaca, New York: Cornell University Press.

Patterson, David. 1995. *Exile: The Sense of Alienation in Modern Russian Letters*. Lexington, Kentucky: University of Press Kentucky.

Peiss, Kathy, Christina Simmons, & Robert Padgug. 1989. *Sexuality in History*. Philadelphia, PA: Temple University Press.

Perec, Georges. 1967. *Les Choses: A Story of the Sixties*. New York: The Grove Press.

Perper, Rosie. 2019. "Mike Pompeo Says its 'Certainly' Possible that Trump May be the Modern-day Savior of the Jewish People". *Business Insider*, March 22. Retrieved October

9, 2019 from www.businessinsider.com/pompeo-says-trump-may-.be-modern-day-jew ish-savior-2019-2013

Petroski, William. 2018. "Iowans Awaiting Trump: 'I Love Him. He is Doing Awesome Things for Our Country'". *Des Moines Register*, October 9. Retrieved November 10, 2019 from www.desmoinesregister.com/story/news/politics/2018/10/09/trump-iowa-polling-voting-election-ethanol-e-15-farmers-republican-reynolds-young-blum-council-bluff/1580599002/

Pezze, Barbara D., & Carlo Salzani. 2009. *Essays on Boredom and Modernity*. New York: Editions Rodopi B.V.

Phillips, Adam. 1993. *On Kissing, Tickling and Being Bored: Psychoanalytic Essays on the Unexamined Life*. USA: Harvard University Press.

Plamper, Jan. 2015. *The History of Emotions: An Introduction*. Oxford: Oxford University Press. https://doi.org/10.1080/00332747.2016.1237742

Poe, Edgar A. 2013. *Literary Life of Thingum Bob, Esq*. USA: Leeaf.com Books.

Porter, Tom. 2017. "Super Putin: Exhibition Depicting Trump's Favorite Russian as Superhero Opens in Moscow". *Newsweek*, December 10. Retrieved December 20, 2019 from www.newsweek.com/super-putin-exhibition-depicting-trumps-favourite-russian-superhero-opens-743663

Power, Carla. 2015. "Terrorists' Most Powerful Recruiting Tool: Boredom". *Time*, May 14. Retrieved December 20, 2019 from https://time.com/3857035/terrorists-recruiting-tool/

Pushkin, Alexander, & James E. Falen. 2009. *Eugene Onegin: A Novel in Verse*. Oxford: Oxford University Press.

Pushkin, Alexander, & Andrey Kneller. 2008. "The Ten Commandments" in *Wondrous Moment: Selected Poetry of Alexander Pushkin*. Boston, MA: Kneller.

Reijseger, Gaby, Wilmar B. Schaufeli, Maria C.W. Peeters, Toon W. Taris, Ilona van Beek, & Else Ouweneel. 2013. "Watching the Paint Dry at Work: Psychometric Examination of the Dutch Boredom Scale". *Anxiety, Stress and Coping* 26(5): 508–525. doi: doi:10.1080/10615806.2012.720676

Richardson, Louise. 2007. *What Terrorists Want: Understanding the Enemy, Containing the Threat*. New York: Random House Trade Paperbacks.

Riesman, David. 2001. *The Lonely Crowd: A Study of the Changing American Character*. USA: Yale University Press.

Rizzo, Salvador, & Meg Kelly. 2018. "Anatomy of a Trump Rally: 76 Percent of Claims are False, Misleading or Lacking Evidence". *The Washington Post*, July 10. Retrieved July 20, 2019 from www.washingtonpost.com/news/fact-checker/wp/2018/07/10/anatomy-of-a-trump-rally-76-percent-of-claims-are-false-misleading-or-lacking-evidence/?noredirect=on&utm_term=.8f5c4dd865df

Roberts, Sarah. 2013. "White Painting [three panel]". San Francisco Museum of Modern Art, July 2013. Retrieved June 3, 2019 from www.sfmoma.org/essay/white-painting-three-panel/

Robinson, Adam. 2018. "Putin Cast as National Saviour Ahead of Russia Election". *BBC News*, January 21. Retrieved March 5, 2018 from www.bbc.com/news/world- europe-42707957

Robinson, W. P. 1975. "Boredom at School". *British Journal of Educational Psychology* (45) 141–152. https://doi.org/10.1111/j.2044-8279.1975.tb03239.x

Rose, Barbara. 1965. "ABC Art", pp. 98–103 in *Boredom*, edited by Tom McDonough, Cambridge, MA: The MIT Press.

Roth, Moira, & Jonathan D. Katz. 2013. *Difference/Indifference: Musings on. Postmodernism, Marcel Duchamp and John Cage*. New York: Routledge. https://doi.org/10.4324/9780203699225

Rothlin, Philippe, & Peter Werder. 2008. *Boreout! Overcoming Workplace Demotivation*. Great Britain & USA: Kogan Page Limited.

Rubin, Jennifer. 2019. "Republicans Accept and Applaud Trump's Horrifying Lies". *The Washington Post*, March 4. Retrieved May 15, 2019 from www.washingtonpost.com/opinions/2019/03/04/lies-republicans-must-believe/?utm_term=.5caa4acba7a1

Russell, Bertrand. 2004. *In Praise of Idleness and Other Essays*. London: Routledge. Classics.

Russell, Bertrand. 2013. *The Conquest of Happiness*. New York: Liveright Publishing Corporation.

Sageman, Marc. 2008. *Leaderless Jihad: Terror Networks in the Twenty-First Century*. Philadelphia, PA: University of Pennsylvania Press.

Schopenhauer, Arthur. 1973. *Essays and Aphorisms*. New York: Penguin Classics.

Schopenhauer, Arthur. 2010. *The Essential Schopenhauer*. New York: Wolfgang Schirmacher.

Schopenhauer, Arthur. 1966. *The World as Will and Representation*. Dover Publications.

Shannon, Claude E., & Warren Weaver. 1949. *The Mathematical Theory of Communication*. Urbana: The University of Illinois Press.

Shaposhnikov, A. K. 2010. Этимёлёгический слёварь сёвременнёгё русскёгё языка. Moscow: Flinta.

Shepherd, Jack. 2017. "John Oliver Enlists Group of Singing Dancers to Warn Donald Trump how 'Ruthless' President Vladimir Putin". *Independent*, February 20. Retrieved October 20 2019 from www.independent.co.uk/arts-.entertainment/tv/news/john-oliver-donald-trump-president-vladimir-putin-singers-dance-pop-song-a7589551.html

Shevstova, Lilia. 2013. *Russia XXI: The Logic of Suicide and Rebirth*. Moscow: Carnegie Endowment for International Peace.

Shevstova, Lilia, & David J. Kramer. 2013. *Crisis: Russia and the West in the Time of Troubles*. Moscow & New York: Carnegie Endowment for International Peace.

Simmel, Georg. 1950. *The Sociology of Georg Simmel*. New York: The Free Press.

Simmel, Georg. 1969. "The Metropolis and Mental Life", pp. 47–60 in *Classic Essays on the Culture of Cities*, edited by R. Sennett, Englewood-Cliffs, NJ: Prentice Hall.

Simmel, Georg. 1986. *Schopenhauer and Nietzsche*. Amherst, MA: The UMASS Press.

Simmel, Georg. 1997. *Simmel on Culture: Selected Writings*. London: SAGE Publications Ltd.

Simmel, Georg. 2011. *The Philosophy of Money*. New York: Routledge Classics.

Simmel, Georg. 2011. *The View of Life: Four Metaphysical Essay with Journal Aphorisms*. Chicago: The University of Chicago Press.

Smith, S., H. Thakurdas, & T. G. Lawes. 1961. "Perceptual Isolation and Schizophrenia". *Journal of Mental Sciences* 107: 839–844. http://10.1192/bjp.107.450.839

Snaith, R. P. 1993. "Identifying Depression: The Significance of Anhedonia". *Hospital Practice* 28 (Sup 5): 55–60. https://doi.org/10.1080/21548331.1993.11442922

Sommer, Barbara. 1985. "What's Different About Truants? A Comparison Study of Eighth- Graders". *Journal of Youth and Adolescence* 5: 411–422. https://doi.org/10.1007/BF02138836

Sontag, Susan. 2002. *Styles of Radical Will*. New York: Picador.

Spacks, Patricia M. 1995. *Boredom: The Literary History of a State of Mind*. Chicago: University of Chicago Press.

Sommers, Jennifer, & Stephen J. Vodanovih. 2000. "Boredom Proneness: Its Relationship to Psychological- and Physical-Health Symptoms". *Journal of Clinical Psychology* 56(1): 149–155. https://doi.org/10.1002/(SICI)1097-4679(200001)56:1<149::AID-JCLP14>3.0.CO;2-Y

Standish, Reid. 2015. "It's Good to Be King: How Putin Spent His 63rd Birthday". *FP*, October 7. Retrieved December 20, 2019 from https://foreignpolicy.com/2015/10/07/its-good-to-be-king-how-putin-spent-his-63rd-birthday/

Stern, Jessica. 2003. *Terror in the Name of God: Why Religious Militants Kill*. New York: Harper Perennial.

Student. 1982. "Boredom". *American Academy of Pediatrics* 70(3): 454.

Suedfeld, Peter, Carmenza Ramirez, & John Deaton. 1982. "Reactions and Attributes of Prisoners in Solitary Confinement". *Criminal Justice and Behavior* 9(3): 303–340. https://doi.org/10.1177/0093854882009003004

Suedfeld, Peter, John W. Turner, & Thomas Fine. 1990. *Restricted Environmental. Stimulation: Theoretical and Empirical Developments in Flotation REST (Recent Research in Psychology)*. New York: Springer-Verlag.

Sundberg, Norman D., Carl A. Latkin, Richard F. Farmer, & Jihad Saoud. 1991. "Boredom in Young Adults: Gender and Cultural Comparisons". *Journal of Cross-Cultural Psychology* 22: 209–223. https://doi.org/10.1177/0022022191222003

Sunkara, Bhaskar. 2019. "The Democratic Debate was Boring. And Centrists were to Blame". *The Guardian*, September 13. Retrieved October 20, 2019 from www.theguardian.com/commentisfree/2019/sep/13/the-democratic-debate-was-boring-and-centrists-were-to-blame

Svendsen, Lars. 2005. *A Philosophy of Boredom*. London: Reaktion Books.

Tabuchi, Hiroko. 2013. "Layoffs Taboo, Japan Workers Are Sent to the Boredom Room". *New York Times*, August 16. Retrieved September 20, 2019 from www.nytimes.com/2013/08/17/business/global/layoffs-illegal-japan-workers-are-sent-to-the-boredom-room.html

Terkel, Studs. 1973. *Working*. New York: Pantheon Books.

Thackray, Richard I. 1981. "The Stress of Boredom and Monotony: A Consideration of the Evidence". *Psychosom Med* 2: 165–176. https://doi.org/10.1097/00006842-198104000-00008

The Moscow Times. 2014. "'No Putin, No Russia,' Says Kremlin Deputy Chief of Staff". *The Moscow Times*, October 23. Retrieved January 20, 2020 from www.themoscowtimes.com/2014/10/23/no-putin-no-russia-says-kremlin-deputy-chief-of-staff-a40702

Tolstoy, Leo. 2002. *Anna Karenina*. New York. Penguin Classics.

Tolstoy, Leo. 2013. *A Short Story Collection: Boredom: The Desire for Desires*. Miniature Masterpieces.

Toohey, Peter. 2011. *Boredom: A Lively History*. London: Yale University Press.

Tornstam, Lars. 2007. "Stereotypes of Old People Persist: A Swedish 'Facts on Aging Quiz' in a 23-year Comparative Perspective". *International Journal of Ageing and Later Life* 1: 33–59. http://10.3384/ijal.1652-8670.072133

Troianovski, Anton. 2020. "Putin Endorses Brazen Remedy to Extend His Rule, Possibly for Life". *The New York Times*, March 10. Retrieved March 10, 2019 from www.nytimes.com/2020/03/10/world/europe/putin-president-russia.html?smid=fbnytimes&smtyp=cur&fbclid=IwAR0FxDXKcxAbaU3bt2GWOIbyfzf0MQUOSre1278id_dLEV8GViOOCS6NVH0

Turgenev, Ivan. 1984. *Diary of a Superfluous Man*. USA: David Patterson.

Udemy Team. 2016. "2016 Udemy Workplace Boredom Study". Udemy for Business, October 26. Retrieved June 2, 2019 from https://about.udemy.com/udemy-for-business/workplace-boredom-study/

United States Census Bureau. 2018. "1860 Census: Population of the United States". Retrieved June 5, 2019 from www.census.gov/library/publications/1864/dec/1860a.html

Uchtmann, Johanna. 2012. "Wenn der Job langweilt, bis der Arzt kommt". *Welt*, January 2. Retrieved January 5, 2019 from www.welt.de/gesundheit/psychologie/article13794240/Wenn-der-Job-langweilt-bis-der-Arzt-kommt.html

Van Putten, Theodore. 1973. "Milieu Therapy: Contraindications?" *Archives of General. Psychiatry* 29: 640–643. http://10.1001/archpsyc.1973.04200050053009

Van Tilburg, Wijnand A. P. 2016. "Going to Political Extremes in Response to Boredom". *European Journal of Social Psychology* 46: 687–699. https://doi.org/10.1002/ejsp.2205

Van Tilburg, Wijnand A. P., & Eric R. Igou. 2011. "On Boredom and Social Identity: A Pragmatic Meaning-Regulation Approach". *Personality and Social Psychology Bulletin* 37: 1679–1691. https://doi.org/10.1177/0146167211418530

Veblen, Thorstein. 2009. *The Theory of the Leisure Class*. Oxford: Oxford University Press.

Wallace, Craig J., Stephen J. Vodanovich, & Becca M. Restino. 2003. "Predicting Cognitive Failures from Boredom Proneness and Daytime Sleepiness Scores: An Investigation within Military and Undergraduate Samples". *Personality and Individual Differences* 34: 635–644. https://doi.org/10.1016/S0191-8869(02)00050–00058

Warhol, Andy, & Pat Hacket. 1980. *POPism: The Warhol '60s*. New York: Harcourt Brace Jovanovich.

Weber, Max. 1978. *Economy and Society*. Berkeley, & Los Angeles, California: University of California Press.

Wegner, Lisa, Alan J. Flisher, Perpetual Chikobvu, Carl Lombard, & Gary King. 2008. "Leisure Boredom and High School Dropout in Cape Town, South Africa. *Journal of Adolescence* 31: 421–431. http://10.1016/j.adolescence.2007.09.004

Weiss, Joanna. 2019. "Trump Pokes Fun at Himself. Why Do Only Some People See It?" *Politico Magazine*, November 9. Retrieved December 5, 2019 from www.politico.com/magazine/story/2019/11/09/trump-pokes-fun-at-himself-why-do-only-some-people-see-it-229908

Wierzbicka, Anna. 1992. *Semantics, Culture, and Cognition: Universal Human Concepts in Culture-Specific Configurations*. New York: Oxford University Press, Inc.

Wilson, Timothy D., David A. Reinhard, Eric C. Westgate, Daniel T. Gilbert, Nicole Ellerbeck, Cheryl Hahn, Casey L. Brown, & Adi Shaked. 2014. "Just Think: The Challenges of the Disengaged Mind". *Science* 345(6192): 75–77. http://10.1126/science.1250830

Wyatt, S. 1929. "Boredom in Industry". *Personnel Journal* 8: 161–171.

Zerubavel, Eviatar. 1981. *Hidden Rythms: Schedules and Calendars in Social Life*. USA: The University of Chicago Press.

Zweig, Ferdynand. 1952. *The British Worker*. Harmondsworth, UK: Pelican.

Index